Using Deliberative Techniques to Teach United States History

Using Deliberative Techniques to Teach United States History

Eleanora von Dehsen, Ph.D.

Nancy Claxton, Ed.D.

International Debate Education Association

New York *Amsterdam*Brussels

Published by

international debate education association

400 West 59th Street
New York, NY 10019

Copyright © 2009 by International Debate Education Association

This work is licensed under the Creative Commons Attribution License:
http://creativecommons.org/licenses/by-nc/3.0/deed.en_US

Activity sheets may be downloaded from www.idebate.org/handouts.htm

Library of Congress Cataloging-in-Publication Data

Dehsen, Eleanora von.
 Using deliberative techniques to teach United States history / Eleanora
von Dehsen, Ph.D., Nancy Claxton, Ed.D.
     p. cm.
 ISBN 978-1-932716-39-9
 1. United States--History--Study and teaching. I. Claxton, Nancy. II. Title.
 E175.8.D447 2009
 973.071--dc22
                                  2009010261

Printed in the United States

 IDEBATE Press

Contents

Introduction

International Debate Education Association (IDEA) believes that free and open discussion is essential to the establishment and preservation of open, democratic societies, and its work supports initiatives promoting excellence and innovation in formal and informal education. IDEA cooperates and maintains contact with educational institutions in over 40 countries. It has extensive experience in conducting teacher training at all levels, as well as in organizing public speaking and debate events for secondary school students through workshops, competitions, and educational institutes. To complement these activities, IDEA has consistently produced quality curricula and educational resources.

Responding to the needs of secondary school teachers in many countries, IDEA has developed deliberative methodology (or deliberative education), which uses interactive teaching and learning approaches—role-play, simulations, debates, speeches, presentations, and so forth—to facilitate learning and create a new form of relationship between you and your class.

Deliberative education methodologies assist teachers in achieving a number of educational goals:
- Fostering interactive instruction, democratic dialogue, student–teacher partnerships, and cooperative learning
- Promoting student ownership of learning and application of knowledge
- Developing students' listening and communication skills
- Developing students' critical thinking and argumentation skills
- Developing students' research (traditional and computer) and critical reading and evaluation skills

Deliberative education is especially suited to the teaching of history, where the goal is not for students simply to learn names, dates, facts, and events, but for them to engage in historical thinking, ask questions, examine the historical record, and research evidence in support of theses. Using deliberative methodology furthers these goals, as it encourages students to analyze, synthesize, and evaluate historical information in order to create and present their own historical arguments and narratives.

DEFINING THE NEED FOR TEACHING HISTORICAL THINKING SKILLS

While most think of facts, dates, people, and events that must be taught when they consider the content of a history curriculum, it is essential to realize that without having the skills to critically analyze these facts, dates, people, and events, history would be incredibly dry in the classroom. It is the study of exploring these details, finding out the whys and hows of events, and trying to make sense of how those details brought us to the world we live in today that brings history to life. Studying history should expect students to query the details, ask thoughtful questions based on their knowledge of events, dates, and people, and collect evidence to answer their own questions.

To truly know history content, students must be encouraged and given opportunities to walk a mile in the shoes of a historical figure who changed their present-day world. They need to try to understand Christopher Columbus's motivations through reading his journals and letters to the king of Spain, or to see through the eyes of an immigrant arriving in the United States on a disease-infested boat from a port in Ireland. These experiences help students to better understand the true price that was paid for the life they enjoy today in the United States, to understand the dark side of our history and where we have learned our lessons, and where we still need to make reforms. To truly think critically about history requires students to engage in guided research and thoughtful discussion, to craft arguments, and to engage in historical role-play. While there are numerous ways to teach content and skills, deliberative methodologies are well-aligned to meet established standards for what students need to know about history.

Reading such narratives requires that students analyze the assumptions—stated and unstated—from which the narrative was constructed, and assess the strength of the evidence presented. It requires that students consider the significance of what the author included as well as chose to omit—the absence, for example, of the voices and experiences of other men and women who were also an important part of the history of their time. Also, this exercise requires that students examine the interpretative nature of history, comparing, for example, alternative historical narratives written by historians who have given different weight to the political, economic, social, and/or technological causes of events and have thereby developed competing interpretations of the significance of those events.

How to Use This Manual

INTEGRATING THIS MATERIAL INTO THE CURRICULUM

Using Deliberative Techniques to Teach United States History is *not* a curriculum. It is a compilation of hands-on instructional approaches that help you to teach required curriculum content in an exciting and thought-provoking way. Deliberative methodology provides an innovative way for you to make key topics in American history come alive in your classroom. You can use the lesson plans as they are presented or modify them to fit your students' needs.

GOALS

The goals of this manual are to use deliberative techniques to advance students' critical thinking skills, specifically historical thinking skills as endorsed by the National Center for History in the Schools, in the five interconnected dimensions of:

1. Chronological Thinking

2. Historical Comprehension

3. Historical Analysis and Interpretation

4. Historical Research Capabilities

5. Historical Issues-Analysis and Decision-Making[1]

The content of this book is based on the National Standards for History for Grades 9–12. The specific topics included were chosen for their importance in the curriculum and because they illustrate the variety of ways you can integrate deliberative methodology into your teaching.

ORGANIZATION

Using Deliberative Techniques to Teach United States History is divided into five chapters:

- Chapter 1 defines deliberative techniques and discusses their uses and benefits in teaching U.S. history content and thinking skills for teachers who are looking for more thought-provoking ways to teach required content. The section presents the various components of the methodology, namely, speeches, presentations, debate, role-play, and simulations.

---

1. National Center for History in the Schools, "Overview of Standards in Historical Thinking" (1996), http://nchs.ucla.edu/standards/thinking5-12.html.

- Chapter 2 looks at important aspects of the colonial experience and the founding of the nation. The first lesson uses writings by Columbus and his contemporaries to help students understand the motives behind exploration and the perceptions explorers had of this "New World." The second lesson asks students to research key colonies so that they can appreciate both their diversity and the experiences and problems they had in common. Lesson 3 explores the importance of imperial policy and the colonial reaction to it that brought about the Revolution. Lesson 4 asks students to analyze the strengths and weaknesses of the Articles of Confederation, while the final lesson in this chapter helps students understand the political theory underlying the Constitution by focusing on the debate surrounding its ratification.

- Chapter 3 surveys the Jacksonian era, growing sectionalism that led to civil war, and Reconstruction. The first lesson in the chapter analyzes the reasons for, and the impact of, Andrew Jackson's policy of Indian Removal. The next lesson utilizes contemporary sources to analyze the debate over slavery. In the third lesson students learn about abolition while exploring the part women played in the movement, along with the contemporary perceptions of women that shaped their role in the abolitionist effort. The fourth lesson uses the Lincoln–Douglas debates to help students understand the growing sectionalism that eventually led to war. The final lesson in the chapter asks students to evaluate and suggest alternatives to Reconstruction.

- Chapter 4 asks students to analyze six key events as the United States emerged as a modern industrial state and faced the Depression and World War II. The chapter begins with a lesson in which students compare and contrast the very different experience of four immigrant groups, as a means of analyzing the impact of nativism, race, and religion on immigration. The second lesson helps students understand Populist and Progressive reform through role-playing individuals prominent at the turn of the 20th century. In the next lesson, students analyze primary documents to understand the reasons for, and opposition to, U.S. entry into World War I. The fourth lesson in this chapter asks students to develop a campaign that will win women the vote. Students then learn about the New Deal and its lasting impact on U.S. government, through an investigation and analysis of Alphabet Agencies. Finally, they debate Truman's decision to use the atomic bomb by examining contemporary arguments.

- Chapter 5 presents lessons that deal with key topics and issues in contemporary America. It begins with an overview of the Rights Revolution, asking students to investigate how the courts, activist organizations, and changing society contributed to the dramatic expansion of civil rights and liberties in the second half of the 20th century. Students next analyze Lyndon Johnson's decision to escalate the Vietnam War. The third lesson in the chapter asks students to debate the relationship between rights and security in wartime. Finally, students are asked to utilize what they have learned to compare life at the beginning of the 20th century with that in contemporary America.

How Do I Find Out More About Deliberative Methodology?

Head straight to Chapter 1 and read on. Here you can find research that backs up deliberative methodology, and how it is best used to teach new concepts. You can present this to your school's instructional leaders to prepare them for all the exciting things that are about to start taking place in your classroom.

How Do I Integrate This Material into the Curriculum I Have to Teach?

Deliberative methodology is a compilation of hands-on instructional approaches—*not* a curriculum. It encourages teachers to teach required curriculum in an exciting and thought-provoking way. The lesson plans in this volume focus on helping students analyze and evaluate 20 key episodes in U.S. history through the use of debate, discussion, presentation, and role-play. Many of the plans also utilize primary documents to further historical thinking. Students, therefore, are required to provide context and analyze the strengths and weaknesses of assumptions in a process that deepens historical understanding. The lessons are written with the assumption that students will already know the basic facts, dates, and events of a topic, and that educators will use the plans to explore subjects in greater depth.

Lesson Organization

Lesson Plans follow a standard format:

    Instructional objectives
    Description
    Time
    Materials
    Preparation (if appropriate)
    Class layout and grouping of students
    Procedure
    Assessment
    Extensions and modifications

This detailed organization helps you plan your lessons and forgo the guesswork typically associated with putting them together. Note the extensions and modifications section is for teachers who want to build on a successful lesson or vary the original lesson plan.

So, if you are ready to get started, head to Chapters 2–5 and start browsing for a lesson plan. Once you teach using deliberative methodology, you will bring the excitement of learning back to life for your students!

Chapter 1
Deliberative Education

DELIBERATIVE EDUCATION DEFINED

Deliberative education is a set of methodologies that employ speech, communication, discussion, and debate in the classroom in order to maximize students' participation in the learning process. Through redefining the role of a teacher in the educational process and challenging students with new tasks, deliberative methodologies engage students in the subject matter by providing an incentive to learn, assisting them in the process of application of knowledge, developing an array of skills, and providing them with a greater ability to adapt to the fast-changing realities of the modern world.

Deliberative education includes a number of educational approaches: educational debates, role-play and simulations, discussions, and individual presentations. Deliberative education is a modern and innovative approach that effectively meets a number of educational goals:

1. Deliberative education engages students in the subject matter by creating an atmosphere conducive to active learning. The traditional educational methodologies are based on a formulaic, top-down method in which students are passive recipients of knowledge passed to them from teachers. Deliberative education is based on democratic dialogues between a teacher and the students, and among students themselves. This methodology opens students to new ways of thinking, allows independent study, promotes problem solving, and encourages free expression of ideas and student creativity. By emphasizing personal investigation and respectful confrontation of different and often opposing ideas in the public but safe setting of a classroom, deliberative education constitutes an educational antidote to the development of passivity and authority dependence among students.

2. Deliberative education offers a holistic and complex approach to learning. Traditional instructional methods are based on a consumer approach to learning, in which knowledge is measured only within the parameters of exam requirements, and it is assumed that students are often not interested in pursuing the depth and complexity of the studied issues. Deliberative education encourages in-depth analysis and examination of complex issues, through researching a variety of sources and reflecting on other areas of knowledge. Deliberative education provides students with an incentive to critically analyze, evaluate, and respond to a variety of issues, thereby preparing them to become engaged and informed citizens in their adult lives.

3. Deliberative education encourages application of attained knowledge. Students engaged in deliberative education become adept at applying the knowledge they have acquired in realistic discussions and debates. Traditional educational methodologies call upon students to display their retention of knowledge through formal exams or tests, simply to prove that they have retained the information, whether it is useful or not. Deliberative education methodologies encourage students to reorganize their knowledge and apply it in different patterns, depending on the context of the learning situation. Deliberative education has its roots in experiential learning, which involves a hands-on approach to teaching and learning. In deliberative education, learners often develop knowledge through a series of discoveries that they themselves direct through practical experience that increasingly progresses in difficulty and thus increases knowledge. Deliberative methodologies prepare students for a variety of roles that they will be expected to assume during their adult life, and provide them with an array of skills necessary in the private, social, and professional spheres of modern society.

4. Deliberative education encourages cooperation and teamwork. Deliberative education shifts teaching and learning from teacher-centered to learner-centered activities. It raises the quality and the amount of active participation among students, and encourages cooperation and sharing of the responsibilities for learning and its outcomes. This method again reflects the demands of the "real world," where individuals most often must work with each other in order to achieve their goals.

5. Deliberative education builds on different learning styles. By confronting students with different tasks, deliberative education meets each student's varying needs, abilities, and learning styles. Deliberative education responds to the needs of those students who focus on feelings and experiences; it responds to the needs of students who value observation and prioritize analysis; and it works well for students who are "doers" and who focus on making links between concepts and their practical applications.

The innovative character of deliberative education is especially useful in the teaching of social sciences, history, civic education, and languages—all subjects where the character and the complexity of studied material requires extended communication, discussion, and deliberation.

Deliberative Methodologies

The most prominent deliberative education methodologies include debate and discussion, simulation and role-play, and individual or group presentation. These deliberative education methodologies can be used either in conjunction with or independently of each other. For example, a chain debate can lead to a debate between two teams, a role-play, or individual or group presentations. Each of these methodologies can be adapted to different subjects, group sizes, and educational goals. A teacher may want to introduce a unit through a simulation exercise and test students' knowledge at the end of a unit through a role-play or parliamentary debate. The options are numerous.

EDUCATIONAL DEBATE

Educational debate is a formal contest of argumentation between two teams, during which one team supports while the other team opposes a given proposition. A debate begins with a "resolution," a simple statement of a topic that is subjected to critical analysis by both teams. The team supporting the resolution speaks first and is referred to as an affirmative team (since it affirms a given resolution). The opposing or "negative" team must then refute the arguments offered by the affirming team and offer arguments against adopting the resolution. Each team is expected not only to outline its positions on a given issue (the so-called cases), but a team is also required to respond directly to the arguments offered by its opponents. It is the job of a "judge," a neutral third party (either an individual or group), to listen carefully to the arguments presented by both sides and decide which set of arguments is most persuasive.

Apart from being an educational methodology, debates have been known as an intrinsic part of democratic institutions since the time of the ancient Greeks. Study and practice of debate furthers the development of skills that are essential to living in a democratic society. Because of this, academic debate has been included in the system of education of many countries (e.g., the United States, Great Britain, and Australia), and thousands of secondary school students all over the world are engaged in debate activities in classrooms and in extracurricular programs. There are many debate formats, which may differ slightly depending on the number of speakers involved in debate (varying usually from two to eight), and their rules and procedure. Debate is a flexible learning tool that meets a number of educational goals. Debate develops communication and speaking skills by providing an opportunity for students to deliver prepared presentations as well as to practice impromptu speaking in response to arguments made by other students. Debate offers structure and imposes limits on speaking order and time, thus introducing an element of control over the process. It develops students' critical thinking skills, both during the process of preparation for debate when students need to develop their team's position on a given issue and during the actual debate when students have to critically respond to others' arguments—thus forcing them to think on their feet. Debate also emphasizes research and the use of written evidence (such as examples and quotes), and requires group work and cooperation among students both during the process of preparation as well as during the debate. Apart from the above-mentioned attributes, debate is an excellent conflict resolution tool that emphasizes peaceful and tolerant communication and respect for the opinions of others.

Debate as a method is best conducted over a number of lessons involving a number of stages: brainstorming and analyzing possible arguments on both sides of the debate; researching a given issue in depth to find supportive and additional arguments; analyzing arguments and preparing teams' cases; the actual debate, during which students present their arguments and respond to the arguments of others; and finally debriefing, in which students can evaluate their performance, consider the outcomes of the debate, and offer feedback to each other.

The teacher's role in debate is best described as coach and facilitator. The teacher should provide a good debate topic, one that will allow the two teams to come up with quality arguments on both sides. The teacher should suggest (or provide) possible resources for researching the topic, and offer guidance during the teams' preparation. Finally, the teacher should judge a debate and offer feedback after the debate is finished.

Debate can involve either a selected number of students (depending on the format) or the whole class. When only some students are directly involved in a given debate, other students should be instructed on how to judge and assess a debate, and offer feedback to their peers.

Although debate is best applied at the end of a unit, providing closure (and being a good test of students' acquisition of knowledge), it can also be used as an introduction to a unit (especially when a debate involves all of the students and aims at testing what students already know about the topic), or during any other stage of educational process on a given unit.

ROLE-PLAY

Role-play is a technique in which students are presented with roles in the form of a case or scenario, and are then asked to act out these roles for educational purposes. Role-play can thus best be described as planned human interaction that involves realistic behavior under artificial or "imagined" conditions. In teaching methodologies, role-play is considered an excellent tool for introducing students to different social roles. Mostly, this process takes place when students are involved in role-play that depicts a specific problem of social life. The goal of role-play as a teaching method is not only to practice competencies but also to stimulate a discussion that allows identification of effective and ineffective patterns of behavior under given circumstances. The technique involves many variations and types. Depending on the level of preparation, these can include spontaneous role-play, dramatic skits, and so on, and on the number of students involved—pairs, groups, and multiple groups. Apart from the functions listed above, in the context of deliberative education, role-play can serve as a method for improving communication, analyzing and researching issues, formulating arguments, and exchanging views on a variety of topics.

Role-play often involves fictitious personae, but teachers may also develop role-play involving real characters, either current or historical figures.

Similar to other deliberative methodologies, role-play develop a number of skills:

- Communication skills—by providing a practical illustration of what happens when people communicate, either verbally or nonverbally; by giving students an opportunity to receive and provide feedback; by developing listening skills through activities that require students to actively listen to each other.

- Research skills—particularly by involving students in more developed and complex role-play that require students to look for sources (on the Internet, in the library); and use the information found effectively, through activities that involve quoting sources and supporting ones' views with relevant data. Research skills also develop an ability to critically evaluate sources through activities involving the assessment of information presented by other students.

- Problem solving and critical thinking skills—by asking students to generate ideas, respond to each others' views, propose alternative solutions, defend their views, and critique the views of others.

Role-play is a highly engaging activity that increases students' participation both during the preparation process and during the activity itself. Role-playing relies heavily on experiences of participants in ways that increase their ownership of learning. Students are engaged in all stages of the role-play, starting with planning, and finishing with debriefing, and as a result students become much more motivated to participate in the process of learning. This technique is highly interactive and shifts teaching and learning from a teacher-centered to a student-centered process.

This technique is also highly flexible. The teacher can change the role-play as it is being conducted, and the materials can be edited to fit particular situations. Role-playing can be engaged in for brief or long periods (some role-play may last as long as 1.5 hours, although 45-minute periods are more common).

Typically, a role-play exercise involves the following stages: introduction, assignment of roles, preparation of the students' groups or individual students, stage preparation (optional), role-play, evaluation, and debriefing.

During the role-play, a teacher should try to exercise a minimum of control, and intervene only to assure the smooth running of a lesson. It is important for teachers to remember that the role-play should be a highly interactive, student-centered activity since only then does it fulfill its educational objectives.

Similar to debate, a role-play can be used during different stages of a particular unit. At the beginning of the unit, it can serve as an excellent introduction and illustration of a certain education point or objective, while a more complex role-play conducted at the end of a unit can serve as a closure and/or a test of students' skills and knowledge.

SIMULATIONS

Simulations are similar to role-play, but they put more emphasis on the process of experiencing interactions and group processes rather than playing individual roles of certain characters (although very often simulations are based on students' playing of certain roles). The difference between the role-play and simulation is also in the authenticity of the roles taken by students. In a simulation exercise students are more likely to play natural roles—that is, roles they sometimes have in real life, while in a role-play they would more often assume roles of fictitious characters.

Simulations develop skills similar to those developed in role-play, while also providing an opportunity to:

- Increase students' awareness of how their perception of others' motivations and cultural heritage can affect their interactions with others. Very often good simulations will lead students to rethink their behavior and attitude toward others;

- Allow students to examine their own biases and focus on how they perceive differences in others, then consider what impact this may have on their interpersonal relations; and

- Allow students to examine how stereotypes are developed and barriers created, and how misunderstandings among people in groups are magnified. Students will also be able to observe, work out, and adopt appropriate mechanisms for successful interactions with others.

Similar to debate and role-play, simulations are excellent teaching methods. They require active participation from students, and they develop strong motivation to learn (especially when an element of competition is introduced). Since most educational simulations present students with a social context in which they have to interact with others, engage in cooperative activities, and later, debrief the process by focusing on their feelings and emotions, a simulation exercise increases students' empathy and teaches the rules of group processes and dynamics.

A well-developed simulation is also conducive to acquiring certain kinds of knowledge, since it allows the participants to learn from personal experiences rather than from a lecture or even a discussion, in which the message is received "secondhand." For example, a cultural diversity simulation will make participants much more sensitive to the fact that cultural differences generate stereotypical perception and thinking than will a lecture on the same subject. Many simulation games will also enable students to develop inquiry skills for gathering information, making inferences, and verifying data. In many simulations, students will need to come up with strategies for solving certain problems or dilemmas, and for achieving certain goals and objectives. This in turn will require the participants to employ their skills in thinking critically, gathering evidence, drawing inferences, making conclusions, and related educational activities.

PRESENTATIONS

Each of the methods presented above will use the element of students' presentations to one degree or another. These presentations will vary in length, level of preparedness, and level of structure and formality. Recognizing the need for students to acquire good presentation skills, not only for the purpose of successful implementation of other deliberative methods but also for more general educational purposes (e.g., making presentations throughout school and college and later in adult life), deliberative education places high emphasis on developing students' presentation skills.

Deliberative education assumes a structured approach to presentations and has developed a range of formats and educational methods to teaching students how to become more effective speakers.

All of the above types of presentations may require students to develop a number of skills and abilities: reasoning and argumentation, organization, style, presentation and delivery (e.g., body language, eye contact, voice, etc.), contact with the audience, and use of presentation aids.

Different types of speeches and presentations share many characteristics, yet teachers may want to emphasize different skills when assigning varying types of speeches. For example, speeches to inform may make greater use of presentation aids than do some speeches made on special occasions.

Teaching of presentation and public speaking can be made part of other deliberative methodologies (e.g., debate) when a teacher emphasizes certain elements of public speaking during the preparation or debriefing process; or these skills can be taught on their own—when teachers ask students to prepare and deliver speeches or presentations on assigned topics or subjects.

Presentations and speeches can be developed into different formats, thereby allowing for individual as well as group work.

Chapter 2
Colonial and Revolutionary Era

This chapter examines important aspects of the colonial experience and the founding of the nation. Students use writings by Columbus and his contemporaries to understand the motives behind exploration and the perceptions explorers had of this "New World." They research key colonies to appreciate both their diversity and the experiences and problems they had in common, and they explore the importance of imperial policy and the colonial reaction to it that brought about the Revolution. Finally, students analyze the strengths and weaknesses of the Articles of Confederation and the political theory underlying the Constitution.

1. In Columbus's Words . . .

INSTRUCTIONAL OBJECTIVES
Students will be able to:
- Articulate Columbus's goals
- Summarize his impressions of the area and peoples he found
- Explain the changes that resulted from his voyages
- Evaluate the long-term significance and impact of his voyages

DESCRIPTION

Students will work in pairs to analyze quotes by Christopher Columbus, in an effort to understand his goals and his impressions of the world he encountered. Students then will analyze the changes in Europe and the Americas that resulted from his exploration, and will discuss the impact Columbus had on both continents.

TIME

60 minutes

MATERIALS

Columbus Quotes (copy for each student)
Impact of Columbus (copy for each student)

CLASS LAYOUT AND GROUPING OF STUDENTS

Students initially will work in pairs, then face their desks toward the center for the discussion.

PROCEDURE

1. Explain that this lesson will focus on Columbus's goals and impressions of the world he encountered and the long-term impact of his exploration.

2. Organize the students into pairs and tell them that first they will work with their partners to analyze a number of quotations from the diaries and letters of Columbus and his son.

3. Distribute Columbus Quotes and ask the students to read through the material and respond to the questions at the end of the activity sheet. They have 20 minutes to prepare for the discussion.

4. After 20 minutes, ask for volunteers to present Columbus's goals and impressions. The goals should include:
   - extending the Catholic faith;
   - finding new sources of trade and profit;
   - establishing a Spanish presence in the newly discovered area.

   Impressions should include:
   - fresh, new, area (later explorers would see it as a reincarnation of the Garden of Eden);
   - a land of gentle people and infinite promise.

   Point out that later explorers would also come with mixed motives, both selfish and exalted. While they hailed the Americas for their purity and promise, they were also willing to take advantage of its innocence.

5. Instruct the students to face their desks toward the center, so they can see all the participants in the discussion. Distribute Impact of Columbus and facilitate a discussion of the long-term influence of Columbus's journeys on the Americas and Europe. Refer to the post-1492 quotes on Columbus Quotes to begin the discussion. Introduce the concept of the Columbian Exchange, the two-way transfers of diseases, plants, animals, and cultures that followed Columbus's voyages. Below are some elements of the exchange:

Americas Received	Europe Received
Diseases: diphtheria, measles, smallpox, and malaria	Diseases: a virulent form of syphilis
Crops and livestock: wheat, rice, coffee, bananas, and olives; horses, cows, pigs, and chickens.	Crops: corn, potatoes, tomatoes, lima beans, squash, peanuts, cassava, cacao, and pineapple; turkey

6. Reread Columbus's assessment of his contribution in his "Letter to Doña Juana de Torres" on the Columbus Quotes sheet. Ask students to respond to this statement in light of the analysis they have just completed on the impact of his journeys.

Assessment
You can assess the students informally during the presentation of goals and impressions as well as during the discussion of impacts.

Extensions and modifications
Have students research the opposition to celebrating Columbus Day in the United States and stage a debate on whether the opposition is valid.

Columbus Quotes

Instructions: Read the following quotes and respond to the questions at the end of the sheet.

CHRISTOPHER COLUMBUS FIRST VOYAGE DIARY 1492

Introduction

Whereas, Most Christian, High, Excellent, and Powerful Princes, King and Queen of Spain . . . this present year 1492, after your Highnesses had terminated the war with the Moors reigning in Europe, . . . and in the present month, in consequence of the information which I had given your Highnesses respecting the countries of India and of a Prince, called Great Can, which in our language signifies King of Kings, how, at many times he, and his predecessors had sent to Rome soliciting instructors who might teach him our holy faith, and the holy Father had never granted his request, whereby great numbers of people were lost, believing in idolatry and doctrines of perdition. Your Highnesses, as Catholic Christians, and princes who love and promote the holy Christian faith, and are enemies of the doctrine of Mahomet, and of all idolatry and heresy, determined to send me, Christopher Columbus, to the above-mentioned countries of India, to see the said princes, people, and territories, and to learn their disposition and the proper method of converting them to our holy faith; and furthermore directed that I should not proceed by land to the East, as is customary, but by a Westerly route, in which direction we have hitherto no certain evidence that any one has gone. So after having expelled the Jews from your dominions, your Highnesses, in the same month of January, ordered me to proceed with a sufficient armament to the said regions of India, and for that purpose granted me great favors, and ennobled me that thenceforth I might call myself Don, and be High Admiral of the Sea, and perpetual Viceroy and Governor in all the islands and continents which I might discover and acquire, or which may hereafter be discovered and acquired in the ocean; and that this dignity should be inherited by my eldest son, and thus descend from degree to degree forever. Hereupon I left the city of Granada, on Saturday, the twelfth day of May, 1492, and proceeded to Palos, a seaport, where I armed three vessels, very fit for such an enterprise, and having provided myself with abundance of stores and seamen, I set sail from the port, on Friday, the third of August, half an hour before sunrise, and steered for the Canary Islands of your Highnesses which are in the said ocean, thence to take my departure and proceed till I arrived at the Indies, and perform the embassy of your Highnesses to the Princes there, and discharge the orders given me. For this purpose I determined to keep an account of the voyage, and to write down punctually every thing we performed or saw from day to day, as will hereafter appear. . . .

October 11, 1492

At two o'clock in the morning the land was discovered, at two leagues' distance; they took in sail and remained under the square-sail lying to till day, which was Friday, when they found themselves near a small island, one of the Lucayos, called in the Indian language Guanahani. Presently they descried people, naked, and the Admiral landed in the boat, which was armed. . . . The Admiral bore the royal standard, and the two captains each a banner of the Green Cross, which all the ships had carried; this contained the initials of the names of the King and Queen each side of the cross, and a crown over each letter. Arrived on shore, they saw trees very green many streams of water, and diverse sorts of fruits.

As I saw that they were very friendly to us, and perceived that they could be much more easily converted to our holy faith by gentle means than by force, I presented them with some red caps, and strings of beads to wear upon the neck, and many other trifles of small value, wherewith they were much delighted, and became wonderfully attached to us. Afterwards they came swimming to the boats, bringing parrots, balls of cotton thread, javelins, and many other things which they exchanged for articles we gave them, such as glass beads, and hawk's bells; which trade was carried on with the utmost good will. But they seemed on the whole to me, to be a very poor people. . . . Weapons they have none, nor are acquainted with them, for I showed them swords which they grasped by the blades, and cut themselves through ignorance. They have no iron, their javelins being without it, and nothing more than sticks, though some have fish-bones or other things at the ends. They are all of a good size and stature, and handsomely formed. . . . It appears to me, that the people are ingenious, and would be good servants and I am of opinion that they would very readily become Christians, as they appear to have no religion. . . .

October 13, 1492

. . . I was very attentive to them, and strove to learn if they had any gold. Seeing some of them with little bits of metal hanging at their noses, I gathered from them by signs that by going southward or steering round the island in that direction, there would be found a king who possessed great cups full of gold. . . . I could conquer the whole of them with fifty men and govern them as I pleased.

October 21, 1492

At 10 o'clock, we arrived at a cape of the island, and anchored, the other vessels in company. After having dispatched a meal, I went ashore, and found no habitation save a single house, and that without an occupant; we had no doubt that the people had fled in terror at our approach, as the house was completely furnished. I suffered nothing to be touched, and went with my captains and some of the crew to view the country. This island even exceeds the others in beauty and fertility. Groves of lofty and flourishing trees are abundant, as also large lakes, surrounded and overhung by the foliage, in a most enchanting manner. Everything looked as green as in April in Andalusia. The melody of the birds was so exquisite that one was never willing to part from the spot, and the flocks of parrots obscured the heavens. The diversity in the appearance of the feathered tribe from those of our country is extremely curious. A thousand different sorts of trees, with their fruit were to be met with, and of a wonderfully delicious odor. It was a great affliction to me to be ignorant of their natures, for I am very certain they are all valuable; specimens of them and of the plants I have preserved. . . . Afterwards I shall set sail for another very large island which I believe to be Cipango, according to the indications I receive from the Indians on board. They call the Island Colba, and say there are many large ships, and sailors there. This other island they name Bosio, and inform me that it is very large; the others which lie in our course, I shall examine on the passage, and according as I find gold or spices in abundance, I shall determine what to do; at all events I am determined to proceed on to the continent, and visit the city of Guisay, where I shall deliver the letters of your Highnesses to the Great Can, and demand an answer, with which I shall return.

Ferdinand Columbus, son of Christopher Columbus, in a diary entry on March 25, 1495

The soldiers mowed down dozens [of Native Americans] with point-blank volleys, loosed the dogs to rip open their limbs and bellies, chased fleeing Indians into the bush to skewer them on sword and pike, and with God's aid soon gained a complete victory, killing many Indians and capturing others who were also killed.

Christopher Columbus 1496 Letter to the Sovereigns, Second Voyage

. . . we can send from here all the slaves and brazilwood which could be sold. . . . In Castile, Portugal, Aragon . . . and the Canary Islands they need many slaves, and I do not think they get enough in Guinea. . . . Although they die now, they will not always die. The Negroes and Canary Islanders died at first.

Letter to Doña Juana de Torres, October 1500

I should be judged as a captain who went from Spain to the Indies to conquer a people numerous and warlike, whose manners and religion are very different from ours, who live in sierras and mountains, without fixed settlements, and where by divine will I have placed under the sovereignty of the King and Queen our Lords, an Other World, whereby Spain, which was reckoned poor, is become the richest of countries.

THE QUESTIONS TO CONSIDER WITH YOUR PARTNER ARE BELOW. HIGHLIGHT
WHICH OF THE QUOTES IN THE PACKET SUPPORT YOUR RESPONSES BELOW.

1. What were Columbus's primary goals?

2. What were Columbus's initial impressions of what he found?

3. What do the post-1492 entries suggest may have happened during the later voyages?

4. How would you evaluate Columbus's own assessment of his exploration?

Sources:

Loewen, James W. *Lies My Teacher Told Me: Everything Your American History Textbook Got Wrong.* Touchstone, 1996.

Mallery, Richard D. *Masterworks of Travel and Exploration.* Ayer Publishing, 1948.

Sale, Kirkpatrick. *Christopher Columbus and the Conquest of Paradise.* Tauris Parke Paperbacks, 2006.

Medieval Sourcebook: *Christopher Columbus: Extracts from Journal.* http://www.fordham.edu/halsall/source/columbus1.html

Copyright ©2009 by International Debate Education Association

The Publisher grants permission for the reproduction of this worksheet except for commercial purposes. Activity sheets may be downloaded from www.idebate.org/handouts.htm

Impact of Columbus

Instructions: Work with the other members of the class to fill in the chart below. Be sure to explore Columbus's impact on the following:

- Native Americans
- Science
- Economy
- Politics
- Cultures
- Daily life

Americas Received		Europe Received	
Before Columbus	After Columbus	Before Columbus	After Columbus

Copyright ©2009 by International Debate Education Association
The Publisher grants permission for the reproduction of this worksheet except for commercial purposes.
Activity sheets may be downloaded from www.idebate.org/handouts.htm

2. The Colonies

INSTRUCTIONAL OBJECTIVES

Students will be able to:

- Compare and analyze how various colonies were established and governed
- Describe the religious and ethnic diversity in the colonies
- Identify and explain the differences among the major economic regions in the colonies
- Determine the problems colonies had in common

DESCRIPTION

Students will work in groups to develop profiles of key colonies, then present their findings to the class. Their analysis will cover the social, religious, and economic life of the colonies, as well as problems the colonies shared.

TIME

60 minutes

MATERIALS

Colonial Overview (copy for each student)

PREPARATION

Reserve the computer lab.

CLASS LAYOUT AND GROUPING OF STUDENTS

Students will work in groups around the computers while researching, then will resume their usual seat assignments for the presentations.

PROCEDURE

1. Explain that the American colonies were diverse. They were settled by different groups of people for different reasons, and they developed in different ways. Some were rural with homogeneous populations; some had towns and were more diverse in their population makeup. Some colonial economies were based on cash crops, others on small farming, and still others on commerce. Some granted more religious freedom than others. Yet they

also had many things in common, including many shared problems. Tell the class that this lesson will explore these differences and similarities.

2. Organize the class into six groups, and name them Massachusetts Bay, Rhode Island, New York, Pennsylvania, Virginia, and North Carolina.

3. Distribute Colonial Overview to the members of each group, and review. Tell the groups to work together using their textbooks and the Internet to develop a profile of their colony and the problems/issues it faced. Give the groups 25 minutes to complete their profiles.

4. Reassemble the class and ask a representative from each colony to present its profile. On the board, create a grid listing colonies and characteristics, and as each colony presents, summarize the findings in the grid. Make sure that each report touches on the kinds of problems the colony faced, and that those reporting on the New England and Middle Colonies have not ignored slavery.

5. Ask the class to review the grid and determine the similarities and differences among the colonies. What were the differences among the three regions: New England, Middle Atlantic, and South? What problems did the colonies have in common? What was most surprising about their findings?

ASSESSMENT
You can assess the students' understanding of the colonies through their colony presentations as well as through the class analysis of similarities and differences.

EXTENSIONS AND MODIFICATIONS
- Have the students role-play residents of each of the colonies—for example, a New England cleric, a Pennsylvania merchant, a Virginia planter—for the purpose of presenting the benefits of their colony to prospective settlers.
- Have the class analyze the importance of slavery in each of the colonies.

Colonial Overview: _____

Instructions: Use your textbooks and the Internet to complete the information requested below for your colony.

Date established:

Purpose of settlement:

Type of colony (charter; proprietary; crown) and government:

Ethnic groups by the time of the Revolution:

Religion and religious freedom:
  Dominant religion

  Established/not established

  Extent of religious freedom

Economy:

Status and importance of slavery:

Important problems/issues (e.g., defense, expansion, internal divisions, relations with royal governor):

Copyright ©2009 by International Debate Education Association
The Publisher grants permission for the reproduction of this worksheet except for commercial purposes.
Activity sheets may be downloaded from www.idebate.org/handouts.htm

3. Revolution!

INSTRUCTIONAL OBJECTIVES

Students will be able to:

- Explain the consequences of the overhaul of British imperial policy following the Seven Years War
- Understand how British policy and the colonial response led to the Revolution

DESCRIPTION

Students will convene as a court of inquiry to report on how key pieces of British legislation— and the colonial response to those measures—led to the break with Great Britain.

TIME

60 minutes

MATERIALS

What Went Wrong? (copy for each student)

PREPARATION

Reserve the computer lab.
Write the following list on the board:

> Sugar Act (1764)
> Stamp Act (1765)
> Quartering Act (1765)
> Declaratory Act (1766)
> Townshend Acts (1767)
> Tea Act (1773)
> Boston Port Act (1774)
> Massachusetts Government Act (1774)
> Administration of Justice Act (1774)
> Quartering Act (1774)
> Quebec Act (1774)

CLASS LAYOUT AND GROUPING OF STUDENTS

Students will work in groups around the computers, and will then convene in their usual seating arrangement for the court of inquiry.

PROCEDURE

1. Explain that the class will be a British court of inquiry convened to investigate the events leading to the American Revolution. The British government wants to know what went wrong and what could have been done—if anything—to prevent American independence, given Britain's colonial policies and goals.

2. Review British colonial policy following the Seven Years War, emphasizing the need to raise revenue and the desire for increased oversight of an ever-more complex empire.

3. Explain that the court is investigating several laws that exacerbated tensions between Britain and the colonies. Tell the class that before they can convene the court, they will work in committees to analyze the impact of each act.

4. Divide the class into 11 groups, distribute "What Went Wrong?" and assign each group a particular act. Tell the groups to use their texts and the Internet to investigate the provisions of the act, reasons for passage, colonial reaction, and British response. They are also to determine why the act was important in the coming of the Revolution, and if the British could have developed a different policy to deal with the situation that had prompted them to enact the law.

5. Once the groups have finished their research, convene the court of inquiry and ask each group to report its findings. The groups should report in chronological order.

6. Ask the court if, in light of the reports, the British government could have done anything to prevent the Revolution.

ASSESSMENT

You can assess the students informally as each group presents its findings and the class discusses the inevitability of the Revolution. Alternatively, you can ask each group to submit its findings for assessment.

EXTENSIONS AND MODIFICATIONS

Debate the statement: British mishandling of colonial affairs and the colonial unwillingness to compromise pushed each side to the brink of war.

What Went Wrong?

Instructions: As part of the government court of inquiry into the causes of the American Revolution, answer the following questions for the act assigned you, and be prepared to present your findings to the court.

Name and date of act:

Provisions:

Reason for passage:

Colonial reaction:

British response:

Why was the act important to the growing rift between Britain and the colonies?

Was an alternative policy available?

Copyright ©2009 by International Debate Education Association
The Publisher grants permission for the reproduction of this worksheet except for commercial purposes.
Activity sheets may be downloaded from www.idebate.org/handouts.htm

4. Articles of Confederation

INSTRUCTIONAL OBJECTIVES

Students will be able to:

- Describe the organization of government under the Articles of Confederation
- Explain the reasons underlying that organization
- Analyze the shortcomings of the Articles
- Understand the reasons for the subsequent convening of the Constitutional Convention

DESCRIPTION

Students will work in groups to examine a summary of the Articles of Confederation, in order to determine the structure and powers of the first national government. Students will use their knowledge of colonial history and the Revolutionary period to understand why the national government was shaped as it was; then they will analyze how the government under the Articles addressed some of the problems facing the new republic.

TIME

60 minutes

MATERIALS

The Articles of Confederation (copy for each student)

Analyzing the Articles (copy for each student)

If you wish the class to read the full text of the Articles of Confederation, direct them to http://www.usconstitution.net/articles.html

CLASS LAYOUT AND GROUPING OF STUDENTS

Students will work in small groups to analyze the Articles, then resume their usual seating arrangements to evaluate the Articles and discuss a series of problems that faced the new government.

PROCEDURE

1. Explain that just days after declaring independence, the Continental Congress established a committee to develop a system of government for the new nation. That system, under the Articles of Confederation, reflected the concerns and experiences of Revolutionary leaders, and was very different from the system eventually adopted under the Constitution. The Articles were in effect from 1781, when the states ratified them, until 1789, after enough states adopted the Constitution for it to go into effect. Tell the class that they will

explore the country's original governing system, the Articles of Confederation, and will analyze the strengths and weaknesses of that document's provisions.

2. Organize the class into groups of four to five and distribute Articles of Confederation and Analyzing the Articles. Tell the students to work in their groups to analyze the articles and answer the questions on the activity sheet. They should be prepared to report back to the class:
    *   Where did power lie under the Articles?
    *   What problems might have arisen from that system?

3. Once the groups have finished their analysis, tell the students to return to their regular seating arrangement. Ask the class to present their findings on state v. national government powers and note these on the board.

4. Facilitate a discussion on where power lay under the Articles and what problems might have arisen from that system. Note the problems on the board.

5. Discuss four problems the nation had to deal with during the Confederation, and ask the students how the national government might have solved them:
    *   Congress must find money to pay debts to veterans as well as private individuals and foreign governments that had loaned the government money during the Revolution.
    *   The British are increasing exports to the United States while keeping U.S. imports to Great Britain to a minimum. Some states erect tariff barriers to limit British imports and force Britain to open its markets.
    *   Both Congress and the states issue paper money. Some state currencies are worth more than others.
    *   Angered by crushing debts and taxes, farmers in western Massachusetts petitioned the state government for relief. When the government failed to adequately respond to their appeals, the farmers, under the leadership of Daniel Shays, resorted to armed protest, posing a serious threat to the Massachusetts government.

6. Explain that the inability of the government to deal with these problems led to growing sentiment in favor of establishing a stronger national government.

ASSESSMENT

You can either assess the students' oral presentations or ask the groups to submit their worksheets for evaluation.

EXTENSIONS AND MODIFICATIONS

Ask the students to use the right-hand column on their resource sheet to note the appropriate provisions of the Constitution. Ask the class to compare the Articles of Confederation and the Constitution and determine the major differences between the two systems.

The Articles of Confederation

Articles of Confederation and perpetual Union between the States of New Hampshire, Massachusetts Bay, Rhode Island and Providence Plantations, Connecticut, New York, New Jersey, Pennsylvania, Delaware, Maryland, Virginia, North Carolina, South Carolina and Georgia.

Article I. The Stile of this Confederacy shall be "The United States of America."

SUMMARY OF PROVISIONS

Legislature	Unicameral Congress	
Appointment of Members	By state legislature as each legislature chooses. (Number of members varies between two and seven per state.)	
Term of office	One year	
Term limits	No more than three out of six years	
Congress paid by	States	
Voting in Congress	One vote per state	
Passing legislation	By majority vote, except for major questions, which require the agreement of nine states	
Executive	None. An annually elected president presides over Congress but has no powers. When Congress is not in session, a Committee of States has the full power of Congress.	
Judiciary	Only maritime judiciary established. Interstate disputes adjudicated by Congress	

Armed forces		
Army	Congress determines size of army and requisitions troops from each state based on population.	
Navy	Congress can build a navy; states can equip warships to fight piracy.	
Foreign affairs	Congress has authority over foreign affairs and the power to make treaties and alliances and to declare war and make peace.	
Coin money	Both the national government and state governments have this power.	
Taxes	Apportioned by Congress; collected by the states. States are asked to, rather than required to, contribute to the national treasury. Congress cannot tax citizens directly.	
Admission of new states	Approval of nine states required.	
Amendment	All states must approve.	
State/federal relations	States keep their sovereignty, freedom, independence, and every power not "expressly delegated" to Congress.	
Ratification	All states must approve.	

Source: U.S. Constitution Online, http://www.usconstitution.net/constconart.html.

Copyright ©2009 by International Debate Education Association
The Publisher grants permission for the reproduction of this worksheet except for commercial purposes. Activity sheets may be downloaded from www.idebate.org/handouts.htm

Analyzing the Articles

Instructions: Use The Articles of Confederation: Summary of Provisions to answer the following questions.

1. The Articles of Confederation established a confederacy. What does that mean? How does this form of government affect the relationship between the states and the national government?

2. Complete the table below, listing what powers the states and national government had under the Articles of Confederation.

STATE V. NATIONAL GOVERNMENT

State Governmental Powers	National Governmental Powers

3. Why do you think the Continental Congress adopted this system?

Be prepared to report to the class:
1. Where did most power lie under this system? (Be prepared to justify your answer.)

2. Present three possible problems with the system.

Copyright ©2009 by International Debate Education Association
The Publisher grants permission for the reproduction of this worksheet except for commercial purposes.
Activity sheets may be downloaded from www.idebate.org/handouts.htm

5. Ratification

INSTRUCTIONAL OBJECTIVES
Students will be able to:
- Understand the issues involved in the ratification of the Constitution
- Assess the arguments of Federalists and Anti-Federalists during the ratification debates

DESCRIPTION

Students will hold a news conference in which Federalists and Anti-Federalists explain their positions to a group of reporters who will question them.

TIME

60 minutes

MATERIALS

Anti-Federalists (copy for each student)
Federalists (copy for each student)
Federalists v. Anti-Federalists (copy for each student)
Ratification Pro and Con (copy for each student) optional

CLASS LAYOUT AND GROUPING OF STUDENTS

Students will work in groups in preparation for the debate. During the news conference, the Federalists and Anti-Federalists will sit at desks facing the reporters.

PROCEDURE

1. Explain that the debates surrounding ratification were intense and split American leaders into two camps: Federalists and Anti-Federalists. Federalists supported a strong national government. They argued that the Constitution would provide the stability and unity missing under the Articles of Confederation, and would facilitate the economic, political, and diplomatic growth of the nation. Anti-Federalists argued that the strong government under the Constitution did not protect basic rights and could lead to tyranny. Anti-Federalists wanted power to reside with the states, whose governments were closer to the people.

2. Tell the class that they will role-play the debate over ratification. Federalists and Anti-Federalists will debate the issue before a group of reporters, who will then ask each side questions.

3. Ask the class to count off into threes: Ones will be Anti-Federalists, Twos will be Federalists, and Threes will be reporters. Have the students assemble in their groups.

4. Distribute Federalists and Anti-Federalists resource sheets and the activity sheet to all students. Explain that these sheets contain writings and speeches from men at the center of the debate:

    Patrick Henry—Revolutionary statesman who declined election to the Constitutional Convention and opposed the Constitution at Virginia's Ratifying Convention.

    Robert Yates and **John Lansing**—New York delegates to the Constitutional Convention who walked out when they sensed that the convention would abandon the Articles of Confederation and propose a new political system with a strong central government. Yates may have been the author of several articles in opposition to the Constitution.

    Elbridge Gerry—Signer of both the Declaration of Independence and the Articles of Confederation. He attended the Constitutional Convention but refused to sign the Constitution.

    James Madison—Often called the Father of the Constitution. He, along with John Jay and Alexander Hamilton, wrote *The Federalist,* a series of articles in defense of the Constitution. These articles had only a slight impact on the contemporary debate but are viewed as the finest defense of the Constitution and a classic in political theory.

    James Wilson—Had a leading role in the Constitutional Convention. His writings and speeches, particularly his speech in the State House Yard, were important in setting the terms of the ratification debate.

5. Ask the class to review the resource sheets, using the material to determine the key issues in the ratification debate. Remind them that, although they will represent only one element in the debate, they must understand both sides of the argument in order to present their strongest case and, in the case of reporters, develop questions.

6. Alternatively, you can omit the documents and distribute Ratification Pro and Con for analysis.

7. Tell the Federalists and Anti-Federalists to develop a short (five-minute) presentation of their case, and to appoint one member of their group to deliver it. The other members will answer reporters' questions. Ask the reporters to develop at least five questions for each side. Remind the reporters that they represent the people, who need a thorough understanding of the issues involved, and therefore these questions should be probing.

8. Once the groups have finished their preparation, organize the class for the conference and ask the Anti-Federalist representative to begin. Reporters are to ask their questions after the Federalists have presented.

9. Make sure that the various members of the two sides, and not the presenters, answer the questions, and that all reporters participate.

10. Point out that a bill of rights was a major concern of many of the states, and that many of the states agreed to ratify the Constitution only after recommending the adoption of such a measure. The Constitution was amended to include the Bill of Rights shortly after the new government was inaugurated.

11. Close by asking the class what the basic concern was underlying the specific arguments of each side. Point out that this basic issue (power of states v. power of federal government) played a central role in the politics of the antebellum period, and that it is still significant.

ASSESSMENT

You can assess the students during the press conference.

EXTENSIONS AND MODIFICATIONS

In Federalist No. 51 James Madison wrote:

> If men were angels, no government would be necessary. If angels were to govern men, neither external nor internal controls on government would be necessary. In framing a government which is to be administered by men over men, the great difficulty lies in this: You must first enable the government to control the governed; and in the next place, oblige it to control itself.

Ask the class whether the Constitution has achieved Madison's goal.

Anti-Federalists

PATRICK HENRY, IN *DEBATE IN THE SEVERAL STATE CONVENTIONS*

The Confederation, this same despised government, merits, in my opinion, the highest encomium. It carried us through a long and dangerous war, it rendered us victorious in that bloody conflict with a powerful nation; it has secured us a territory greater than any European monarch possesses; and shall a government which has been thus strong and vigorous, be accused of imbecility and want of energy? Consider what you are about to do before you part with the government . . . Similar examples are to be found in ancient Greece and ancient Rome—instances of the people losing their liberty by their own carelessness, and the ambition of a few. We are cautioned by the honorable gentleman who presides, against faction and turbulence. I acknowledge that licentiousness [excess] is dangerous, and that it ought to be provided against; I acknowledge also, the new form of government may effectually prevent it; yet there is another thing it will as effectually do—it will oppress and ruin the people.

. . . Such a government is incompatible with the genius of republicanism. There will be no checks, no real balances. . . . But, sir, we are not feared by foreigners; we do not make nations tremble. Would this constitute happiness or secure liberty?

. . . Go to the poor man and ask him what he does. He will inform you that he enjoys the fruits of his labor, under his own fig tree, with his wife and children around him, in peace and security. . . . Why then, tell us of dangers, to terrify us into an adoption of this new form of government?

This constitution is said to have beautiful features, but when I come to examine these features, sir, they appear to me horribly frightful: among other deformities it has an awful squinting; it squints towards monarchy... Your president may easily become king: your senate is so imperfectly constructed that your dearest rights may be sacrificed by what may be a small minority....

If your American chief be a man of ambition and abilities, how easy it is for him to render himself absolute.... Away with your president, we shall have a king; the army will salute him monarch; your militia will leave you and assist in making him king, and fight against you.

. . .

Our rights and privileges are endangered, and the sovereignty of the state will be relinquished; and cannot we plainly see that this is actually the case? The rights of conscience, trial by jury, liberty of the press, all your immunities and franchise, all pretensions to human rights and privileges are rendered insecure, if not lost, by this change.

... If you give up these powers without a bill of rights you will exhibit the most absurd thing to mankind that ever the world saw—a government that has abandoned all its powers—the powers of a direct taxation, the sword and the purse. You have disposed of them to congress, without a bill of rights—without check, limitation, or control.

Source: Bernard Feder, *Viewpoints USA* (American Book Company, 1967), pp. 55, 56.

ROBERT YATES AND JOHN LANSING, IN *DEBATE IN THE SEVERAL STATE CONVENTIONS*

... we entertained an opinion that a general government, however guarded by declarations of rights, or cautionary provisions, must unavoidably, in a short time be productive of the destruction of the civil liberty of such citizens who could be effectually coerced by it, by reason of the extensive territory of the United States, the dispersed situation of its inhabitants, and the insuperable difficulty of controlling or counteracting the views of a set of men (however unconstitutional and oppressive their acts may be) possessed of all the powers of government and who, from their remoteness from their constituents, and necessary permanence of office, could not be supposed to be uniformly actuated by an attention to their welfare and happiness; that however wise and energetic the principles of the general government might be, the extremities of the United states could not be kept in due submission and obedience to its laws, at the distance of many hundred miles from the seat of government; that if so numerous a body of men as to represent the interests of all the inhabitants of the United States in the usual and true ideas of representation, the expense of supporting it would be intolerable.

Source: Bernard Feder, *Viewpoints USA* (American Book Company, 1967), pp. 57–58.

Elbridge Gerry, Letter to the Speaker of the Massachusetts state legislature, October 18, 1787

Gentlemen:

I have the honor to enclose, pursuant to my commission, the Constitution proposed by the Federal Convention.

To this system I gave my dissent, and shall submit my objections to the honorable legislature.

It was painful for me, on a subject of such national importance, to differ from the respectable members who signed the Constitution; but conceiving, as I did, that the liberties of America were not secured by the system, it was my duty to oppose it.

My principal objections to the plan are, that there is no adequate provision for a representation of the people; that they have no security for the right of election; that some of the powers of the legislature are ambiguous, and others indefinite and dangerous; that the executive is blended with, and will have an undue influence over, the legislature; that the judicial department will be oppressive; that treaties of the highest importance may be formed by the President, with the advice of two thirds of a quorum of the Senate; and that the system is without the security of a bill of rights. These are objections which are not local, but apply equally to all the states.

As the Convention was called for "the sole and express purpose of revising the Articles of Confederation, and reporting to Congress, and the several legislatures, such alterations and provisions as shall render the Federal Constitution adequate to the exigencies of government, and the preservation of the Union," I did not conceive that these powers extend to the formation of the plan proposed; but the Convention being of a different opinion, I acquiesced in it, being fully convinced that, to preserve the Union, an efficient government was indispensably necessary, and that it would be difficult to make proper amendments to the Articles of Confederation.

The Constitution proposed has few, if any, federal features, but is rather a system of national government. Nevertheless, in many respects, I think it has great merit, and, by proper amendments, may be adapted to the "exigencies of government, and preservation of liberty."

The question on this plan involves others of the highest importance: 1. Whether there shall be a dissolution of the federal government; 2. Whether the several state governments shall be so altered as in effect to be dissolved; 3. Whether, in lieu of the federal and state governments, the national Constitution now proposed shall be substituted without amendment. Never, perhaps, were a people called on to decide a question of greater magnitude. Should the citizens of America adopt the plan as it now stands, their liberties may be lost; or should they reject it altogether, anarchy may ensue. It is evident, therefore, that they should not be precipitate in their decisions; that the subject should be well understood;—lest they should refuse to support the government after having hastily accepted it.

If those who are in favor of the Constitution, as well as those who are against it, should preserve moderation, their discussions may afford much information, and finally direct to a happy issue.

It may be urged by some, that an implicit confidence should be placed in the Convention; but, however respectable the members may be who signed the Constitution, it must be admitted that a free people are the proper guardians of their rights and liberties; that the greatest men may err, and that their errors are sometimes of the greatest magnitude.

Others may suppose that the Constitution may be safely adopted, because therein provision is made to amend it. But cannot this object be better attained before a ratification than after it? And should a free people adopt a form of government under conviction that it wants amendment?

And some may conceive that, if the plan is not accepted by the people, they will not unite in another. But surely, while they have the power to amend, they are not under the necessity of rejecting it.

I have been detained here longer than I expected, but shall leave this place in a day or two for Massachusetts, and on my arrival shall submit the reasons (if required by the legislature) on which my objections are grounded.

I shall only add that, as the welfare of the Union requires a better Constitution than the Confederation, I shall think it my duty, as a citizen of Massachusetts, to support that which shall be finally adopted, sincerely hoping it will secure the liberty and happiness of America.

I have the honor to be, gentlemen, with the highest respect for the honorable legislature and yourselves, your most obedient and very humble servant,

Source: Library of Congress, American Memory, http://memory.loc.gov/learn/features/timeline/newnatn/usconst/egerry.html.

Federalists

JAMES MADISON, "FEDERALIST 10"

Among the numerous advantages promised by a well-constructed Union, none deserves to be more accurately developed than its tendency to break and control the violence of faction. . . . Complaints are everywhere heard from our most considerate and virtuous citizens, . . . that our governments are too unstable, that the public good is disregarded in the conflicts of rival parties, and that measures are too often decided, not according to the rules of justice and the right of the minor party, but by the superior force of an interested and overbearing majority.

. . . that the most common and durable source of factions [party rivalry] has been the various and unequal distribution of property. Those who hold and those who are without property have ever formed distinct interests in society. Those who are creditors and those who are debtors, fall under a like discrimination. A landed interest, a moneyed interest, with many lesser interests, grow up of necessity in civilized nations, and divide them into different classes actuated by different sentiments and views. The regulation of these various and interfering interests forms the principal task of modern legislation, and involves the spirit of party and faction in the necessary and ordinary operations of the government. . . .

. . . it may be concluded that a pure democracy . . . can admit of no cure for the mischief of faction. . . . A republic . . . promises the cure for which we are seeking. . . .

The effect is . . . to refine and enlarge the public views, by passing them through the medium of a chosen body of citizens, whose wisdom may best discern the true interest of their country. . . . On the other hand, . . . men of factious tempers of local prejudices . . . may . . . betray the interests of the people. . . . The influence of factious leaders may kindle a flame within their particular States, but will be unable to spread a general conflagration through the other States. . . .

Source: Bernard Feder, *Viewpoints USA* (American Book Company, 1967), p. 58.

JAMES WILSON, SPEECH TO THE PENNSYLVANIA LEGISLATURE (STATE HOUSE YARD SPEECH) OCTOBER 6, 1787

It will be proper . . . to mark the leading discrimination between the State constitutions and the constitution of the United States. When the people established the powers of legislation under their separate governments, they invested their representatives with every right and authority which they did not in explicit terms reserve; and therefore upon every question respecting the jurisdiction of the House of Assembly, if the frame of government is silent, the jurisdiction is efficient and complete. But in delegating federal powers, another criterion was necessarily introduced, and the congressional power is to be collected, not from tacit implication, but from the positive grant expressed in the instrument of the union. Hence, it is evident, that in the former case everything which is not reserved is given; but in the latter the reverse of the proposition prevails, and everything which is not given is reserved.

This distinction being recognized, will furnish an answer to those who think the omission of a bill of rights a defect in the proposed constitution; for it would have been superfluous and absurd to have stipulated with a federal body of our own creation, that we should enjoy those privileges of which we are not divested, either by the intention or the act that has brought the body into existence. For instance, the liberty of the press, which has been a copious source of declamation and opposition—what control can proceed from the

Federal government to shackle or destroy that sacred palladium of national freedom? . . . In truth, then, the proposed system possesses no influence whatever upon the press, and it would have been merely nugatory to have introduced a formal declaration upon the subject—nay, that very declaration might have been construed to imply that some degree of power was given, since we undertook to define its extent.

. . .

This constitution, it has been further urged, is of a pernicious tendency, because it tolerates a standing army in the time of peace. This has always been a topic of popular declamation; and yet I do not know a nation in the world which has not found it necessary and useful to maintain the appearance of strength in a season of the most profound tranquility. Nor is it a novelty with us; for under the present articles of confederation, Congress certainly possesses this reprobated power, and the exercise of that power is proved at this moment by her cantonments along the banks of the Ohio. But what would be our national situation were it otherwise? Every principle of policy must be subverted, and the government must declare war, before they are prepared to carry it on. Whatever may be the provocation, however important the object in view, and however necessary dispatch and secrecy may be, still the declaration must precede the preparation, and the enemy will be informed of your intention, not only before you are equipped for an attack, but even before you are fortified for a defence. The consequence is too obvious to require any further delineation, and no man who regards the dignity and safety of his country can deny the necessity of a military force, under the control and with the restrictions which the new constitution provides.

Perhaps there never was a charge made with less reasons than that which predicts the institution of a baneful aristocracy in the federal Senate. This body branches into two characters, the one legislative and the other executive. In its legislative character it can effect no purpose, without the co-operation of the House of Representatives, and in its executive character it can accomplish no object without the concurrence of the President. Thus fettered I do not know

any act which the Senate can of itself perform, and such dependence necessarily precludes every idea of influence and superiority. But I will confess that
in the organization of this body a compromise between contending interests
is descernible; and when we reflect how various are the laws commerce,
habits, population and extent of the confederated States, this evidence of mu-
tual concession and accommodation ought rather to command a generous
applause, than to excite jealousy and reproach. For my part, my admiration
can only be equalled by my astonishment in beholding so perfect a system
formed from such heterogeneous materials.

The next accusation I shall consider is that which represents the federal constitution, as not only calculated, but designedly framed, to reduce the State
governments to mere corporations and eventually to annihilate them. Those
who have employed the term corporation upon this occasion are not perhaps
aware of its extent. In common parlance, indeed, it is generally applied to
petty associations for the ease and convenience of a few individuals; but in
its enlarged sense, it will comprehend the government of Pennsylvania, the
existing union of the States, and even this projected system is nothing more
than a formal act of incorporation. But upon what presence can it be alleged
that it was designed to annihilate the State governments? For I will undertake
to prove that upon their existence depends the existence of the Federal plan.
For this purpose, permit me to call your attention to the manner in which the
President, Senate and House of Representatives are proposed to be appointed.
The President is to be chosen by electors, nominated in such manner as the
legislature of each State may direct; so that if there is no legislature there can
be no electors, and consequently the office of President cannot be supplied.

The Senate is to be composed of two Senators from each State, chosen by
the Legislature; and, therefore, if there is no Legislature, there can be no Senate. The House of Representatives is to be composed of members chosen
every second year by the people of the several States, and the electors in each
State shall have the qualifications requisite for electors of the most numerous
branch of the State Legislature; unless, therefore, there is a State Legislature,
that qualification cannot be ascertained, and the popular branch of the fed-

eral constitution must be extinct. From this view, then, it is evidently absurd to suppose that the annihilation of the separate governments will result from their union; or, that having that intention, the authors of the new system would have bound their connection with such indissoluble ties. Let me here advert to an arrangement highly advantageous, for you will perceive, without prejudice to the powers of the Legislature in the election of Senators, the people at large will acquire an additional privilege in returning members to the House of Representatives; whereas, by the present confederation, it is the Legislature alone that appoints the delegates to Congress.

The power of direct taxation has likewise been treated as an improper delegation to the federal government; but when we consider it as the duty of that body to provide for the national safety, to support the dignity of the union, and to discharge the debts contracted upon the collected faith of the States for their common benefit, it must be acknowledged that those upon whom such important obligations are imposed, ought in justice and in policy to possess every means requisite for a faithful performance of their trust. But why should we be alarmed with visionary evils? I will venture to predict that the great revenue of the United States must, and always will, be raised by impost, for, being at once less obnoxious and more productive, the interest of the government will be best promoted by the accommodation of the people. Still, however, the objects of direct taxation should be within reach in all cases of emergency; and there is no more reason to apprehend oppression in the mode of collecting a revenue from this resource, than in the form of an impost, which by universal assent, is left to the authority of the federal government. In either case, the force of civil institutions will be adequate to the purpose; and the dread of military violence, which has been assiduously disseminated, must eventually prove the mere effusion of a wild imagination or a factious spirit. But the salutary consequences that must flow from thus enabling the government to receive and support the credit of the union, will afford another answer to the objections upon this ground. The State of Pennsylvania particularly, which has encumbered itself with the assumption of a great proportion of the public debt, will derive considerable relief and advantage, for, as it was the imbecility of the present confederation which gave rise to the funding law, that law must naturally expire, when a competent and energetic federal system shall be substituted—the State will then be discharged from an extraordinary burthen, and the national creditor will find it to be his interest to return to his original security.

After all, my fellow-citizens, it is neither extraordinary or unexpected that the constitution offered to your consideration should meet with opposition. It is the nature of man to pursue his own interest in preference to the public good, and I do not mean to make any personal reflection when I add that it is the interest of a very numerous, powerful and respectable body to counteract and destroy the excellent work produced by the late convention. All the officers of government and all the appointments for the administration of justice and the collection of the public revenue which are transferred from the individual to the aggregate sovereignty of the States, will necessarily turn the stream of influence and emolument into a new channel. Every person, therefore, who enjoys or expects to enjoy a place of profit under the present establishment, will object to the proposed innovation; not, in truth, because it is injurious to the liberties of his country, but because it affects his schemes of wealth and consequence. I will confess, indeed, that I am not a blind admirer of this plan of government, and that there are some parts of it which, if my wish had pre-vailed, would certainly have been altered. But when I reflect how widely men differ in their opinions, and that every man (and the observation applies like-wise to every State) has an equal pretension to assert his own, I am satisfied that anything nearer to perfection could not have been accomplished. If there are errors, it should be remembered that the seeds of reformation are sown in the work itself and the concurrence of two-thirds of the Congress may at any time introduce alterations and amendments. Regarding it, then, in every point of view, with a candid and disinterested mind, I am bold to assert that it is the best form of government which has ever been offered to the world.

Source: Constitution Society, http://www.constitution.org/afp/jwilson0.htm.

Ratification Pro and Con

Anti-Federalist (con)	Federalists (pro)
The Confederation served us well. It is strong, having seen us through a war with the most powerful nation on Earth.	The Confederation is weak. Without a strong government, instability and anarchy are always a threat. We have seen this in recent events such as Shays' Rebellion, in the increasing disputes between states, and in the economic problems caused by the lack of a strong government.
The Constitution has established a consolidated government, not a federal one. The vast powers given to the central government weaken state governments by stripping them of many powers. Because republics can exist only in small, homogenous territories, the United States must maintain its confederate structure, where the states are the dominant powers. The United States is too large for a federal system.	The Constitution has established a federal, not a consolidated government, in which the states and a central authority share power.
A centralized republic will not work in a large country with so many varied interests. Citizens cannot keep a watchful eye on their representatives.	A large federal republic is better able to resist factionalism that may endanger the rights of a minority. With so many interests, it will be difficult to develop a majority united in a purpose that might endanger a minority.

Anti-Federalist (con)	Federalists (pro)
Congress holds too much power, as can be evidenced in Article 1 of the Constitution: "The Congress shall have Power. . .To make all Laws which shall be necessary and proper for carrying into Execution the foregoing Powers, and all other Powers vested by this Constitution in the Government of the United States, or in any Department or Officer thereof."	The "necessary and proper clause" is not a grant of ultimate power but a declaration that Congress possesses all the means necessary to carry out its specifically granted powers—not abuse those it already has. The federal judiciary will interpret the Constitution and so curb any attempt of Congress to increase its powers beyond the Constitution's scope.
Congress has far too much economic and political power, particularly the power of the purse and sword. Direct taxation is a form of coercion and, given our colonial experience, the fact that the Constitution does not outlaw standing armies is troubling.	Congress needs the power both to assess taxes and to collect them. We must pay down the large continental debt in order to foster economic growth. A standing army will protect America from foreign invasion and domestic insurrections.
The President is far too strong, and his veto and pardoning powers are monarchical. He could become a king.	We need a strong executive to conduct foreign policy and enforce laws. Checks and balances will prevent tyranny. The President is accountable to the people for reelection, and Congress can impeach, convict, and remove him. Under the Constitution, power is distributed among three independent branches of the government. Because all three are equal in power, no one branch can assume control over another.

Anti-Federalist (con)	Federalists (pro)
The Senate will become an aristocracy. Since its members are not chosen directly by the people [until the ratification of the Seventeenth Amendment in 1913 state legislatures chose senators], they do not necessarily have to be responsive to the will of the people. The blending of the powers of the President and Senate, especially on appointments and treaties, is especially troubling.	As James Madison has said, the Senate is necessary as a "defense to the people [represented in the House] against their own temporary errors." It will blend "stability with liberty." The House of Representatives will serve as a check on the Senate in the legislature, while the Senate must work with the president in the executive arena.
Most important, the Constitution lacks a bill of rights protecting individuals against the encroachments of this strong national government. We must have guarantees of freedom of religion, press, and speech; the right to bear arms; jury trials in civil and criminal cases; freedom against unwarranted searches and seizures; and the right of petition and assembly.	Although necessary in a monarchy, a bill of rights is not needed in a republic where the people rule. The Constitution gives Congress only strictly delegated powers; all other powers are reserved to the states. If Congress has no authority in areas where a bill of rights is important (such as freedom of religion, press, etc.), a bill is not necessary. Further, to simply create a list of rights can be dangerous. Are people then only limited to the rights included in the list? As it is not feasible or logical to list all the rights, it is better to list none at all.

Copyright ©2009 by International Debate Education Association
The Publisher grants permission for the reproduction of this worksheet except for commercial purposes.
Activity sheets may be downloaded from www.idebate.org/handouts.htm

Chapter 3
Expansion, Reform, and Unification

In this chapter students explore three significant issues in the antebellum era: Indian Removal, the push for social reform, and the debate over slavery. The lesson on Indian Removal helps students understand how some of the major forces underlying the politics of the period, including westward expansion, the debate over government powers, and racism, impacted government policy. The next two lessons focus on the debate over slavery and explore the part women played in the abolition movement. The fourth lesson uses the Lincoln–Douglas debates to help students understand the growing sectionalism that eventually led to war, while the final lesson asks students to evaluate Reconstruction.

6. Indian Removal

INSTRUCTIONAL OBJECTIVES

Students will be able to:

- Understand Jacksonian Indian policy
- Analyze the impact of removal and resettlement on the Cherokee, Chickasaw, Choctaw, and Seminole tribes

DESCRIPTION

Students will take part in a panel-discussion role-play, with a group of students acting as representatives of the Jackson administration and other groups playing Native Americans from the different tribes most affected by Jackson's Indian removal policies. They will discuss the impact of the removal on their tribes and will then analyze Jackson's policy in the broader context of westward expansion and government powers.

TIME

60 minutes

MATERIALS

Trail of Tears (copy for each student)
Indian Removal Act of 1830 (copy for each student)
Five Tribes (copy for each representative)
Andrew Jackson and the U.S. Government (copy for each representative)

PREPARATION

Reserve computer lab.

CLASS LAYOUT AND GROUPING OF STUDENTS

Students will begin in the usual classroom arrangement. They will then do research in groups around the computers. For the panel discussion, arrange the desks so that the representatives of the U.S. government face the representatives of the Five Tribes.

PROCEDURE

1. Explain that during the 1830s the U.S. government, under President Andrew Jackson, forced the removal of the Five Civilized Tribes to Indian Territory in a brutal migration known as the Trail of Tears. The class will hold a panel discussion exploring the government's Indian policy and the Five Tribes' experience. They will then analyze the policy in the broader context of westward migration and the role and powers of the U.S. government during that period.

2. Provide an overview of the events leading up to Indian Removal, emphasizing the following:
   - Indian policy was determined by two conflicting goals: fair treatment of the Native Americans and promotion of the western movement of American settlers, with the former invariably subordinate to the latter.
   - Initial efforts to deal with increased tensions between Indians and settlers by a policy of assimilation failed, leading to emphasis on removal.
   - Removal was cloaked in legality through the use of treaties.
   - Election of legendary Indian fighter Andrew Jackson to the presidency seals the fate of the tribes.

   (You can find an excellent overview of removal at http://www.digitalhistory.uh.edu/database/article_display_printable.cfm?HHID=638/.)

3. Explain that for the panel discussion, students will take on the role of members of one of the Five Tribes or of Jackson and the U.S. Government. Divide the class into the six groups:
   - Jackson and the U.S. Government
   - Cherokee
   - Chickasaw
   - Choctaw
   - Creek
   - Seminole

4. Distribute Trail of Tears and Indian Removal Act of 1830 to all students, and Five Tribes and Andrew Jackson and the U.S. Government to the appropriate groups. Tell each group to research its stand on and experience with Indian Removal and prepare a short presentation of their findings. (Groups can elect a spokesperson or divide portions of the presentation.)

5. Answer any questions the students may have about their task and allow them to begin. Circulate to answer any questions and to ensure students are on task.

6. After 25 minutes, ask the students to reassemble their desks so that they can hold a panel discussion with chairs at the front for the U.S. government representatives and chairs facing the panel for the various tribe representatives.

7. Ask Andrew Jackson and the U.S. Government to provide a brief overview of their role and experience. Then call on the Tribes.

8. Once the groups have finished their presentations, lead a discussion of the policy. You may wish the class to respond to the following statement from the overview essay cited in the activity sheets:

> Even had the federal government wanted to, it probably lacked the resources and military means necessary to protect the eastern Indians from encroaching white farmers, squatters, traders, and speculators. . . . Removal failed in large part because of the nation's commitment to limited government and its lack of experience with social welfare programs. Contracts for food, clothing, and transportation were awarded to the lowest bidders, many of whom failed to fulfill their contractual responsibilities. Indians were resettled on semi-arid lands, unsuited for intensive farming. The tragic outcome was readily foreseeable.

> (Source: Digital History, http://www.digitalhistory.uh.edu/database/article_display_printable.cfm?HHID=638)

9. Conclude by noting that in 1841 the federal government ordered Maj. Ethan Allen Hitchcock to conduct an inquiry into the Trail of Tears. His honest investigation reported that before, during, and after removal "bribery, perjury, and forgery, short weights, issues of soiled meat and grain, and every conceivable subterfuge was employed by designing white men." The federal government decided not to make the report public.

ASSESSMENT
You can assess the students informally during their presentations and discussion. Alternatively, you can ask the students to prepare written reports on the experience of their groups.

EXTENSIONS AND MODIFICATIONS
Explore and debate the legal argument surrounding the Cherokee tribe's challenge to removal.

Trail of Tears

Nation	Population east of the Mississippi before removal treaty	Removal treaty (year signed)	Years of major emigration	Total number emigrated or forcibly removed	Deaths during removal
Choctaw	19,554	Dancing Rabbit Creek (1830)	1831–1836	12,500	2,000–4,000+
Creek	22,700 + 900 black slaves	Cusseta (1832)	1834–1837	19,600	3,500
Chickasaw	4,914 + 1,156 black slaves	Pontotoc Creek (1832)	1837–1847	4,000 +	Figure unavailable
Cherokee	21,500 + 2,000 black slaves	New Echota (1835)	1836–1838	20,000 + 2,000 slaves	2,000–8,000
Seminole	5,000 + fugitive slaves	Payne's Landing (1832)	1832–1842	2,833	Figure unavailable

Source: Grant Foreman, *Indian Removal: The Emigration of the Five Civilized Tribes of Indians* (University of Oklahoma Press, 1932, 1989).

Indian Removal Act 1830

CHAP. CXLVIII.—*An Act to provide for an exchange of lands with the Indians residing in any of the states or territories, and for their removal west of the river Mississippi.*

SEC. 1. *Be it enacted by the Senate and House of Representatives of the United States of America, in Congress assembled*, That it shall and may be lawful for the President of the United States to cause so much of any territory belonging to the United States, west of the river Mississippi, not included in any state or organized territory, and to which the Indian title has been extinguished, as he may judge necessary, to be divided into a suitable number of districts, for the reception of such tribes or nations of Indians as may choose to exchange the lands where they now reside, and remove there; and to cause each of said districts to be so described by natural or artificial marks, as to be easily distinguished from every other.

SEC. 2. *And be it further enacted*, That it shall and may be lawful for the President to exchange any or all of such districts, so to be laid off and described, with any tribe or nation of Indians now residing within the limits of any of the states or territories, and with which the United States have existing treaties, for the whole or any part or portion of the territory claimed and occupied by such tribe or nations, within the bounds of any one or more of the states or territories, where the land claimed and occupied by the Indians, is owned by the United States, or the United States are bound to the state within which it lies to extinguish the Indian claim thereto.

SEC. 3. *And be it further enacted*, That in the making of any such exchange or exchanges, it shall and may be lawful for the President solemnly to assure the tribe or nation with which the exchange is made, that the United States will forever secure and guaranty to them, and their heirs or successors, the country so exchanged with them; and if they prefer it, that the United States will cause a patent or grant to be made and executed to them for the same: *Provided always*, That such lands shall revert to the United States, if the Indians become extinct, or abandon the same.

SEC. 4. *And be it further enacted*, That if, upon any of the lands now occupied by the Indians, and to be exchanged for, there should be such improvements as add value to the land claimed by any individual or individuals of such tribes or nations, it shall and may be lawful for the President to cause such value to be ascertained by appraisement or otherwise, and to cause such ascertained value to be paid to the person or persons rightfully claiming such improvements. And upon the payment of such valuation, the improvements so valued and paid for, shall pass to the United States, and possession shall not afterwards be permitted to any of the same tribe.

SEC. 5. *And be it further enacted*, That upon the making of any such exchange as is contemplated by this act, it shall and may be lawful for the President to cause such aid and assistance to be furnished to the emigrants as may be necessary and proper to enable them to remove to, and settle in, the country for which they may have exchanged; and also, to give them such aid and assistance as may be necessary for their support and subsistence for the first year after their removal.

SEC. 6. *And be it further enacted*, That it shall and may be lawful for the President to cause such tribe or nation to be protected, at their new residence, against all interruption or disturbance from any other tribe or nation of Indians, or from any other person or persons whatever.

SEC. 7. *And be it further enacted*, That it shall and may be lawful for the President to have the same superintendence and care over any tribe or nation in the country to which they may remove, as contemplated by this act, that he is now authorized to have over them at their present places of residence: *Provided*, That nothing in this act contained shall be construed as authorizing or directing the violation of any existing treaty between the United States and any of the Indian tribes.

SEC. 8. *And be it further enacted*, That for the purpose of giving effect to the provisions of this act, the sum of five hundred thousand dollars is hereby appropriated, to be paid out of any money in the treasury, not otherwise appropriated.

APPROVED

Five Civilized Tribes

Instructions: Use the following websites to gain an overview of Indian Removal and research the experience of your assigned tribe. Answer the questions below to help your group prepare a short presentation of the tribes' experience for the panel discussion.

SOURCES

Overview of Removal:
http://www.digitalhistory.uh.edu/database/article_display_printable.cfm?HHID=638/.

Cherokee:
http://www.arkansasheritage.com/in_the_classroom/lesson_plans/american_indian/
cherokee_lesson_plan01-10-2003.pdf.

Chickasaw:
http://www.arkansasheritage.com/in_the_classroom/lesson_plans/american_indian/
chicksaw.pdf.

Choctaw:
http://www.arkansasheritage.com/in_the_classroom/lesson_plans/american_indian/
choctaw.pdf.

Creek:
http://www.arkansasheritage.com/in_the_classroom/lesson_plans/american_indian/
creek.pdf.

Seminole:
http://www.arkansasheritage.com/in_the_classroom/lesson_plans/american_indian/
seminole.pdf.

QUESTIONS

1. What efforts did the nation undertake to resist removal?

2. How did the government get the tribe to agree to removal?

3. What was the tribe's experience during removal?

4. How did the tribe fare in Indian territory?

Copyright ©2009 by International Debate Education Association
The Publisher grants permission for the reproduction of this worksheet except for commercial purposes.
Activity sheets may be downloaded from www.idebate.org/handouts.htm

Andrew Jackson and the U.S. Government

Instructions: Go to the following website for an overview of Indian Removal:

http://www.digitalhistory.uh.edu/database/article_display_printable.cfm?HHID=638

Then, read the following excerpts from Andrew Jackson's speeches and answer the questions below to prepare a short presentation for the panel discussion.

ANDREW JACKSON ON INDIAN POLICY (1829)

It will be my sincere and constant desire to observe toward the Indian tribes within our limits a just and liberal policy, and to give that humane and considerate attention to their rights and their wants which is consistent to the habits of our Government and the feelings of our people.

Source: First Inaugural Address, http://www.synaptic.bc.ca/ejournal/ JacksonFirstInauguralAddress.htm.

ANDREW JACKSON'S CASE FOR THE REMOVAL ACT, 1830

It gives me pleasure to announce to Congress that the benevolent policy of the Government, steadily pursued for nearly thirty years, in relation to the removal of the Indians beyond the white settlements is approaching to a happy consummation. Two important tribes have accepted the provision made for their removal at the last session of Congress, and it is believed that their example will induce the remaining tribes also to seek the same obvious advantages.

The consequences of a speedy removal will be important to the United States, to individual States, and to the Indians themselves. The pecuniary advantages which it Promises to the Government are the least of its recommendations. It puts an end to all possible danger of collision between the authorities of the General and State Governments on account of the Indians. It will place a dense and civilized population in large tracts of country now occupied by a few savage hunters. By opening the whole territory between Tennessee on the north and Louisiana on the south to the settlement of the whites it will incalculably strengthen the southwestern frontier and render the adjacent States strong enough to repel future invasions without remote aid. It will relieve the whole State of Mississippi and the western part of Alabama of Indian occupancy, and enable those States to advance rapidly in population, wealth, and power. It will separate the Indians from immediate contact with settlements of whites; free them from the power of the States; enable them to pursue happiness in their own way and under their own rude institutions; will retard the progress of decay, which is lessening their numbers, and perhaps cause them gradually, under the protection of the Government and through the influence of good counsels, to cast off their savage habits and become an interesting, civilized, and Christian community. These consequences, some of them so certain and the rest so probable, make the complete execution of the plan sanctioned by Congress at their last session an object of much solicitude.

Toward the aborigines of the country no one can indulge a more friendly feeling than myself, or would go further in attempting to reclaim them from their wandering habits and make them a happy, prosperous people. I have endeavored to impress upon them my own solemn convictions of the duties and powers of the General Government in relation to the State authorities. For the justice of the laws passed by the States within the scope of their reserved powers they are not responsible to this Government. As individuals we may entertain and express our opinions of their acts, but as a Government we have as little right to control them as we have to prescribe laws for other nations.

. . .

Humanity has often wept over the fate of the aborigines of this country, and Philanthropy has been long busily employed in devising means to avert it, but its progress has never for a moment been arrested, and one by one have many powerful tribes disappeared from the earth. To follow to the tomb the last of his race and to tread on the graves of extinct nations excite melancholy reflections. But true philanthropy reconciles the mind to these vicissitudes as it does to the extinction of one generation to make room for another. In the monuments and fortresses of an unknown people, spread over the extensive regions of the West, we behold the memorials of a once powerful race, which was exterminated or has disappeared to make room for the existing savage tribes. Nor is there anything in this which, upon a comprehensive view of the general interests of the human race, is to be regretted. Philanthropy could not wish to see this continent restored to the conditions in which it was found by our forefathers. What good man would prefer a country covered with forests and ranged by a few thousand savages to our extensive Republic, studded with cities, towns, and prosperous farms, embellished with all the improvements which art can devise or industry execute, occupied by more than 12,000,000 happy people, and filled with all the blessings of liberty, civilization, and religion?

The present policy of the Government is but a continuation of the same progressive change by a milder process. The tribes which occupied the countries now constituting the Eastern States were annihilated or have melted away to make room for the whites. The waves of population and civilization are rolling to the westward, and we now propose to acquire the countries occupied by the red men of the South and West by a fair exchange, and, at the expense of the United States, to send them to a land where their existence may be prolonged and perhaps made perpetual. Doubtless it will be painful to leave the graves of their fathers; but what do they more than our ancestors did or than our children are now doing? To better their condition in an unknown land our forefathers left all that was dear in earthly objects. Our children by thousands yearly leave the land of their birth to seek new homes in distant regions. Does Humanity weep at these painful separations from everything, animate and inanimate, with which the young heart has become entwined? Far from it. It is rather a source of joy that our country affords scope where our young population may range unconstrained in body or in mind, developing the power and faculties of man in their highest perfection. These remove hundreds and almost thousands of miles at their own expense, purchase the lands they occupy, and support themselves at their new homes from the moment of their arrival. Can it be cruel in this Government when, by events which it can not control, the Indian is made discontented in his ancient home to purchase his lands, to give him a new and extensive territory, to pay the expense of his removal, and support him a year in his new abode? How many thousands of our own people would gladly embrace the opportunity of removing to the West on such conditions! If the offers made to the Indians were extended to them, they would be hailed with gratitude and joy.

And is it supposed that the wandering savage has a stronger attachment to his home than the settled, civilized Christian? Is it more afflicting to him to leave the graves of his fathers than it is to our brothers and children? Rightly considered, the policy of the General Government toward the red man is not only liberal, but generous. He is unwilling to submit to the laws of the States and mingle with their population. To save him from this alternative, or perhaps utter annihilation, the General Government kindly offers him a new home, and proposes to pay the whole expense of his removal and settlement. . . .

May we not hope, therefore, that all good citizens, and none more zealously than those who think the Indians oppressed by subjection to the laws of the States, will unite in attempting to open the eyes of those children of the forest to their true condition, and by a speedy removal to relieve them from all the evils, real or imaginary, present or prospective, with which they may be supposed to be threatened.

Source: First Annual Message to Congress, http://www.mtholyoke.edu/acad/intrel/andrew.htm.

Andrew Jackson: Removal of Southern Indians (1835)

The plan of removing the aboriginal people who yet remain within the settled portions of the United States to the country west of the Mississippi River approaches its consummation. It was adopted on the most mature consideration of the condition of this race, and ought to be persisted in till the object is accomplished, and prosecuted with as much vigor as a just regard to their circumstances will permit, and as fast as their consent can be obtained. All preceding experiments for the improvement of the Indians have failed. It seems now to be an established fact that they can not live in contact with a civilized community and prosper. Ages of fruitless endeavors have at length brought us to a knowledge of this principle of intercommunication with them. The past we can not recall, but the future we can provide for. Independently of the treaty stipulations into which we have entered with the various tribes for the usufructuary rights they have ceded to us, no one can doubt the moral duty of the Government of the United States to protect and if possible to preserve and perpetuate the scattered remnants of this race which are left within our borders. In the discharge of this duty an extensive region in the West has been assigned for their permanent residence. It has been divided into districts and allotted among them. Many have already removed and others are preparing to go, and with the exception of two small bands living in Ohio and Indiana, not exceeding 1,500 persons, and of the Cherokees, all the tribes on the east side of the Mississippi, and extending from Lake Michigan to Florida, have entered into engagements which will lead to their transplantation.

The plan for their removal and reestablishment is founded upon the knowledge we have gained of their character and habits, and has been dictated by a spirit of enlarged liberality. A territory exceeding in extent that relinquished has been granted to each tribe. Of its climate, fertility, and capacity to support an Indian population the representations are highly favorable. To these districts the Indians are removed at the expense of the United States, and with certain supplies of clothing, arms, ammunition, and other indispensable articles; they are also furnished gratuitously with provisions for the period of a year after their arrival at their new homes. In that time, from the nature of the country and of the products raised by them, they can subsist themselves by agricultural labor, if they choose to resort to that mode of life; if they do not they are upon the skirts of the great prairies, where countless herds of buffalo roam, and a short time suffices to adapt their own habits to the changes which a change of the animals destined for their food may require. Ample arrangements have also been made for the support of schools; in some instances council houses and churches are to be erected, dwellings constructed for the chiefs, and mills for common use. Funds have been set apart for the maintenance of the poor; the most necessary mechanical arts have been introduced, and blacksmiths, gunsmiths, wheelwrights, millwrights, etc., are supported among them. Steel and iron, and sometimes salt, are purchased for them, and plows and other farming utensils, domestic animals, looms, spinning wheels, cards, etc., are presented to them. And besides these beneficial arrangements, annuities are in all cases paid, amounting in some instances to more than $30 for each individual of the tribe, and in all cases sufficiently great, if justly divided and prudently expended, to enable them, in addition to their own exertions, to live comfortably. And as a stimulus for exertion, it is now provided by law that "in all cases of the appointment of interpreters or other persons employed for the benefit of the Indians a preference shall be given to persons of Indian descent, if such can be found who are properly qualified for the discharge of the duties."

Such are the arrangements for the physical comfort and for the moral improvement of the Indians. The necessary measures for their political advancement and for their separation from our citizens have not been neglected. The pledge of the United States has been given by Congress that the country destined for the residence of this people shall be forever "secured and guaranteed to them." A country west of Missouri and Arkansas has been assigned to them, into which the white settlements are not to be pushed. No political communities can be formed in that extensive region, except those which are established by the Indians themselves or by the United States for them and with their concurrence. A barrier has thus been raised for their protection against the encroachment of our citizens, and guarding the Indians as far as possible from those evils which have brought them to their present condition. Summary authority has been given by law to destroy all ardent spirits found in their country, without waiting the doubtful result and slow process of a legal seizure. I consider the absolute and unconditional interdiction of this article among these people as the first and great step in their melioration. Halfway measures will answer no purpose. These can not successfully contend against the cupidity of the seller and the overpowering appetite of the buyer. And the destructive effects of the traffic are marked in every page of the history of our Indian intercourse.

Some general legislation seems necessary for the regulation of the relations which will exist in this new state of things between the Government and people of the United States and these transplanted Indian tribes, and for the establishment among the latter, and with their own consent, of some principles of intercommunication which their juxtaposition will call for; that moral may be substituted for physical force, the authority of a few and simple laws for the tomahawk, and that an end may be put to those bloody wars whose prosecution seems to have made part of their social system.

After the further details of this arrangement are completed, with a very general supervision over them, they ought to be left to the progress of events. These, I indulge the hope, will secure their prosperity and improvement, and a large portion of the moral debt we owe them will then be paid.

Source: Extract from Jackson's Seventh Annual Message to Congress. Facts On File. American Indian History Online, http://www.fofweb.com/NuHistory/default.asp?ItemID=WE43&NewItemID=True/.

QUESTIONS

1. How did Jackson characterize his views toward Indians? How would you characterize them?

2. On what grounds did Jackson justify his removal policy?

3. What benefits did he see for the U.S. government and the states from removal?

4. What benefits did he see for American settlers?

5. What benefits did he see for the Five Tribes?

6. What provisions did he make for the Five Tribes as they moved?

7. Did his administration accomplish all of the goals of his Indian policy?

Copyright ©2009 by International Debate Education Association
The Publisher grants permission for the reproduction of this worksheet except for commercial purposes.
Activity sheets may be downloaded from www.idebate.org/handouts.htm

7. Slavery

INSTRUCTIONAL OBJECTIVES
Students will be able to:
- Explain the reasons given for and against slavery
- Explain how differences over the morality and legitimacy of slavery heightened the sectional crisis in the antebellum period

DESCRIPTION

Students will use contemporary sources, some of which they will find offensive, to understand opposing views on slavery. They will work in small groups to analyze arguments for and against "the peculiar institution." They will then explore how these different attitudes toward slavery contributed to the sectional crisis.

TIME

60 minutes

MATERIALS

Two Views of Slavery (copies for each student)
Opposing Arguments on Slavery (copies for each student)

CLASS LAYOUT AND GROUPING OF STUDENTS

Students will begin the lesson in their usual seating assignments and then break into small groups to analyze the contemporary documents. They will resume their usual seats for the discussion.

PROCEDURE

1. Explain that in the years prior to the Civil War the nation engaged in a vigorous debate over slavery. Many in the North opposed the institution on moral and economic grounds, while many in the South viewed it as, in the words of John C. Calhoun, a "positive good." Tell the class that this lesson will explore both sides of the argument. Warn them that they will find some of what they will be reading offensive, but that the excerpts reflect the thinking of the day.

2. Distribute Two Views of Slavery. Ask the students to read the selection and then discuss.

3. Organize the class into six groups:
   1. Proslavery Morality Arguments
   2. Proslavery Religious Arguments
   3. Proslavery Economic Arguments
   4. Antislavery Morality Arguments
   5. Antislavery Religious Arguments
   6. Antislavery Economic Arguments

   Distribute Opposing Arguments on Slavery. Ask each group to analyze the documents on the two resource sheets to find their specific arguments and prepare a short presentation of those arguments for the class.

4. Reassemble the class and ask a representative from each group to present their findings.

5. Facilitate a short discussion of whether, given the different attitudes over slavery, sectional conflict was inevitable? Was the North willing to risk disintegration of the Union over emancipation? Was there any room for compromise? (You may wish to direct the discussion to the Great Compromises of the era and their fate.)

6. Point out that as a result of growing antislavery sentiment in the North and the stridency of abolitionists such as Garrison, the South became a closed society. Postmasters refused to deliver antislavery literature, and debate about slavery was forbidden. Ask the class what effect Southern action may have had on sectional tensions.

7. Close by reminding students that while Southern attitudes toward blacks and arguments in support of slavery are abhorrent to us today, the North was not innocent. Institutionalized racism pervaded that region.

ASSESSMENT
You can informally assess the students during the discussion, and as they summarize their arguments.

EXTENSIONS AND MODIFICATIONS
Ask the class to explore the biographies and writings of key abolitionists. Then debate whether these writings and actions helped or hindered the abolitionists' cause.

Two Views of Slavery

GEORGE FITZHUGH, "THE UNIVERSAL LAW OF SLAVERY"

He the Negro is but a grown up child, and must be governed as a child, not as a lunatic or criminal. The master occupies toward him the place of parent or guardian. . . .

Secondly, The negro is improvident; . . . will not accumulate in youth for the exigencies of age. He would become an insufferable burden to society. Society has the right to prevent this, and can only do so by subjecting him to domestic slavery. In the last place, the negro race is inferior to the white race, and living in their midst, they would be far outstripped or outwitted in the chaos of free competition. Gradual but certain extermination would be their fate. . . .

We would remind those who . . . sympathize with negro slavery, that his slavery here relieves him from a far more cruel slavery in Africa, or from idolatry and cannibalism, and every brutal vice and crime that can disgrace humanity, and that it Christianizes, protects, supports. . . .

The negro slaves of the South are the happiest, and, in some sense, the freest people in the world. The children and the aged and infirm work not at all, and yet have all the comforts and necessaries of life provided for them. They enjoy liberty, because they are oppressed neither by care nor labor. The women do little hard work, and are protected from the despotism of their husbands by their masters. The negro men and stout boys work, on average in good weather, not more than nine hours a day. The balance of their time is spent in perfect abandon. Besides' they have their Sabbaths and holidays. White men, with so much of license and liberty, would die of ennui; but negroes luxuriate in corporal and mental repose. . . .

A common charge preferred against slavery is, that it induces idleness in the masters. . . . If they do their duty, their time is fully occupied. If they do not, the estate goes to ruin. . . . The master labors for the slave, they exchange industrial value. But the capitalist, living on his income, gives nothing to his subjects. He lives by mere exploitation.

Source: http://www.pbs.org/wgbh/aia/part4/4h3141t.html.

Theodore D. Weld, "Slavery As It Is"

Two million seven hundred thousand persons in these States are . . . slaves and are held such by force, and by being put in fear, and this for no crime! Reader, what have you to say of such treatment? . . . Suppose I should seize you, rob you of your liberty; drive you into the field and make you work without pay as long as you live. . . .

We will prove that the slaves in the United States are treated with barbarous inhumanity; that they are overworked, underfed, wretchedly clad and lodged, and have insufficient sleep; that they are often made to wear round their necks iron collars armed with prongs, to drag heavy chains and weights at their feet while working in the field, and to wear yokes, and bells, and iron horns; that they are often confined in the stocks day and night . . . that they are frequently flogged with terrible severity.

We will show, not merely that such deeds are committed, but that they are frequent . . . not in one of the slave states, but in all of them.

Source: Bernard Feder, *Viewpoints USA* (American Book Company, 1967), pp. 123–124.

Opposing Arguments on Slavery

JOHN C. CALHOUN, *A DISQUISITION ON GOVERNMENT*

It is a great and dangerous error to suppose that all people are equally entitled to liberty. It is a reward to be earned, not a blessing to be gratuitously lavished on all alike; —a reward reserved for the intelligent, the patriotic, the virtuous and deserving; —and not a boon to be bestowed on a people too ignorant, degraded and vicious to be capable either of appreciating it or of enjoying it. . . .

These great and dangerous errors have their origin in the prevalent opinion that all men are born free and equal;—than which nothing can be more un-founded and false . . . men, . . . instead of being born free and equal, are born subject, not only to parental authority, but to the laws and institutions of the county where born, and under whose protection they draw their first breath.

Source: Bernard Feder, *Viewpoints USA* (American Book Company, 1967), p. 128

WILLIAM LLOYD GARRISON, SELECTIONS FROM WRITINGS AND SPEECHES

More than fifty-seven years have elapsed, since a band of patriots convened in this place to devise measures for the deliverance of this country from a foreign yoke. The corner-stone on which they founded the Temple of Freedom was broadly this—"that all men are created equal; that they are endowed by their Creator with certain inalienable rights; that among these are life, LIBERTY, and the pursuit of happiness." At the sound of their trumpet-call, three millions of people rose up as from the sleep of death, and rushed to the strife of blood; deeming it more glorious to die instantly as freemen, than desiring to live one hour as slaves. . . .

. . . those, for whose emancipation we are striving—constituting at the present time at least one-sixth of their countrymen . . . really enjoy no constitutional nor legal projection. . . .

We . . . maintain—That no man has a right to enslave or imbrute his brother—to hold or acknowledge him, for one moment, as a piece of merchandise—to keep back his hire by fraud—or to brutalize his mind by denying him the means of intellectual, social and moral improvement.

Source: Bernard Feder, *Viewpoints USA* (American Book Company, 1967), p. 127

James H. Hammond, "On the Admission of Kansas" 1858

In all social systems there must be a class to do the menial duties, to perform the drudgery of life. That is, a class requiring but a low order of intellect and but little skill. Its requisites are vigor, docility, fidelity. Such a class you must have, or you would not have that other class which leads progress, civilization, and refinement. It constitutes the very mud-sill of society and of political government; and you might as well attempt to build a house in the air, as to build either the one or the other, except on this mud-sill. Fortunately for the South, she found a race adapted to that purpose to her hand. A race inferior to her own, but eminently qualified in temper, in vigor, in docility, in capacity to stand the climate, to answer all her purposes. We use them for our purpose, and call them slaves. . . . I will not characterize that class at the North with that term; but you have it; it is there; it is everywhere; it is eternal.

The Senator from New York said yesterday that the whole world had abolished slavery. Aye, the *name*, but not the *thing*; all the powers of the earth cannot abolish that. God only can do it when he repeals the *fiat*, "the poor ye always have with you;" for the man who lives by daily labor, and scarcely lives at that, and who has to put out his labor in the market, and take the best he can get for it; in short, your whole class of manual laborers and "operatives," as you call them, are essentially slaves. The difference between us is, that our slaves are hired for life and well compensated; there is no starvation, no begging, no want to employment among our people, and not too much employment either. Yours are hired by the day, not cared for, and scantily compensated, which may be proved in the most painful manner, at any hour in any street in any of your large towns. . . . Our slaves are black, of another and inferior race. The *status* in which we have placed them is an elevation. . . . They are happy, content, unaspiring, and utterly incapable, from the intellectual weakness, ever to give us any trouble by their aspirations. Yours are white, of your own race; you are brothers of one blood. They are your equals in natural endowment of intellect, and they feel galled by their degradation. Our slaves do not vote. We give them not political power. Yours do vote, and being the majority, they are the depositaries of all your political power. If they knew the tremendous secret, that the ballot-box is stronger than "an army with banners," and could combine, where would you be? Your society would be reconstructed, your government overthrown. . . .

Source: http://dig.lib.niu.edu/teachers/econ1-hammond.html.

ABRAHAM LINCOLN, SPEECH AT NEW HAVEN, 1860

When one starts poor, as most do in the race of life, free society is such that he knows he can better his condition; he knows that there is no fixed condition of labor for his whole life. . . . I want every man to have a chance—and I believe a black man is entitled to it—in which he can better his condition—when he may look forward and hope to be a hired laborer this year and the next, work for himself afterwards, and finally to hire men to work for him. . . .

Source: Bernard Feder, *Viewpoints USA* (American Book Company, 1967), p. 125.

Thomas R. Dew, An Essay On Slavery, 1832

It is said slavery is wrong, in the *abstract* at least, and contrary to the spirit of Christianity. To this we answer . . . that any question must be determined by its circumstances, and if, as really is the case, we cannot get rid of slavery without producing a greater injury to both the masters and slaves, there is no rule of conscience or revealed law of God which *can* condemn us. . . .

With regard to the assertion that slavery is against the spirit of Christianity, we are ready to admit the general assertion, but deny most positively that there is anything in the Old or New Testament which would go to show that slavery, when once introduced, ought at all events to be abrogated, or that the master commits any offense in holding slaves. The children of Israel themselves were slaveholders and were not condemned for it. All the patriarchs themselves were slaveholders. . . . When the children of Israel conquered the land of Canaan, they made one whole tribe "hewers of wood and drawers of water," and they were at that very time under the special guidance of Jehovah; they were permitted expressly to purchase slaves of the heathen and keep them as an inheritance for their posterity; and even the children of Israel might be enslaved for six years.

When we turn to the New Testament, we find [not] one single passage at all calculated to disturb the conscience of an honest slaveholder. No one can read it without seeing and admiring that the meek and humble Saviour of the world in no instance meddled with the established institutions of mankind; he came to save a fallen work, and not to excite the black passions of man and array them in deadly hostility against each other. From no one did he turn away; his plan was offered alike to all—to the monarch and the subject, the rich and the poor, the master and the slave. He was born in the Roman world, a world in which the most galling slavery existed, a thousand times more cruel than the slavery in our own country; and yet he nowhere encourages insurrection, he nowhere fosters discontent; but exhorts *always* to implicit obedience and fidelity.

What a rebuke does the practice of the Redeemer of mankind imply upon the conduct of some of his nominal disciples of the day, who seek to destroy the contentment of the slave, to rouse their most deadly passions, to break up the deep foundations of society, and to lead on to a night of darkness and confusion! "Let every man," (says Paul) "abide in the same calling wherein he is called. Art thou called *being* a servant? Care not for it; but if thou mayest be made free, use *it* rather" (I *Corinth. vii.* 20,21). . . . Servants are even commanded in Scripture to be faithful and obedient to unkind masters. "Servants," (says Peter) "be subject to your masters with all fear; not only to the good and gentle but to the forward. For what glory is it if when ye shall be buffeted for your faults ye take it patiently; but if when ye do will and suffer for it, yet take it patiently, this is acceptable with God" (I *Peter ii.* 18,20). These and many other passages in the New Testament most convincingly prove that slavery in the Roman world was nowhere charged as a fault or crime upon the holder, and everywhere is the most implicit obedience enjoined.

We beg leave . . . to address a few remarks to those who have conscientious scruples about the holding of slaves, and therefore consider themselves under an obligation to break all the ties of friendship and kindred—dissolve all the associations of happier days to flee to a land where this evil does not exist. We cannot condemn the conscientious actions of mankind, but we must be permitted to say that if the assumption even of these pious gentlemen be correct, we do consider their conduct as very unphilosophical; and we will go further still: we look upon it as even immoral upon their own principles.

Let us admit that slavery is an evil; and what then? Why, it has been entailed upon us by no fault of ours, and must we shrink from the charges which devolves upon us, and throw the slave, in consequence, unto those hands of those who have no scruples of conscience—those who will not perhaps treat him so kindly? No! This is not philosophy, it is not morality; . . .

Look to the slaveholding population of our country and you everywhere find them characterized by noble and elevated sentiments, by humane and virtuous feelings. We do not find among them that cold, contracted, calculating *selfishness,* which withers and repels everything around it, and lessens or destroys all the multiplied enjoyments of social intercourse. Go into our national councils and ask for the most generous, the most disinterested, the most conscientious, and the least unjust and oppressive in their principles, and see whether the slaveholder will be passed by in the selection. . . .

Source: http://www.wwnorton.com/college/history/archive/resources/documents/ch15_03.htm.

ABRAHAM LINCOLN FRAGMENT ON SLAVERY, 1858

Suppose it is true, that the negro is inferior to the white, in the gifts of nature; is it not the exact reverse justice that the white should, for that reason, take from the negro, any part of the little which has been given him? "Give to him that is needy" is the Christian rule of charity; but "Take from him that is needy" is the rule of slavery.

PRO-SLAVERY THEOLOGY

The sum of pro-slavery theology seems to be this: "Slavery is not universally right, nor yet universally wrong; it is better for some people to be slaves; and, in such cases, it is the Will of God that they be such."

Certainly there is no contending against the Will of God; but still there is some difficulty in ascertaining, and applying it, to particular cases. For instance we will suppose the Rev. Dr. Ross has a slave named Sambo, and the question is "Is it the Will of God that Sambo shall remain a slave, or be set free?" The Almighty gives no audable [sic] answer to the question, and his revelation—the Bible— gives none—or, at most, none but such as admits of a squabble, as to it's [sic] meaning. No one thinks of asking Sambo's opinion on it. So, at last, it comes to this, that Dr. Ross is to decide the question. And while he consider [sic] it, he sits in the shade, with gloves on his hands, and subsists on the bread that Sambo is earning in the burning sun. If he decides that God wills Sambo to continue a slave, he thereby retains his own comfortable position; but if he decides that God wills Sambo to be free, he thereby has to walk out of the shade, throw off his gloves, and delve for his own bread. Will Dr. Ross be actuated by that perfect impartiality, which has ever been considered most favorable to correct decisions?

But, slavery is good for some people!!! As a good thing, slavery is strikingly perculiar [sic], in this, that it is the only good thing which no man ever seeks the good of, for himself.

Nonsense! Wolves devouring lambs, not because it is good for their own greedy maws, but because it is good for the lambs!!!

Source: http://www.teachingamericanhistory.org/library/index.
asp?document=783/.

8. Women and Abolition

INSTRUCTIONAL OBJECTIVES

Students will be able to:

- Understand the broader political context in which abolitionism developed
- Understand the position of women in antebellum society
- Understand the position of women in the abolitionist movement

DESCRIPTION

Students will work in teams to analyze a historical document in order to understand the position of women in antebellum society and their role in the abolitionist movement.

TIME

60 minutes

MATERIALS

What Have Women to Do with Slavery? (copy for each student)

CLASS LAYOUT AND GROUPING OF STUDENTS

Students will work in small groups and then reassemble in their usual seating arrangement to discuss their findings.

PROCEDURE

1. Explain that the years 1820–1860 were known as the Age of Reform, during which Americans launched unprecedented reforms to aid the sick and mentally ill, rehabilitate criminals, improve education, promote temperance, further women's rights, and end slavery.

2. Present a short summary of the forces behind reform, emphasizing:
    - Religion, particularly the Second Great Awakening
    - The Declaration of Independence
    - The Enlightenment's faith in reason

3. Explain that women were very active in the reforms of the period, but that when they sought to involve themselves in those reform efforts, they became aware of the limitations society placed on them. Tell the class that they will analyze a historical document that illustrates both women's place in reform and the problems they encountered.

4. Divide the class into groups of four and distribute What Have Women to Do with Slavery? Tell the class to read the dialogue and work together in their groups to answer the questions on the activity sheet in preparation for a class discussion.

5. Answer any questions the students may have and allow them to begin. Circulate to address any further questions and to ensure that students are on task.

6. Once the groups have finished their analysis, reassemble the class and ask for volunteers to answer the questions. Then lead a discussion of attitudes toward women during the period.

7. Conclude by telling students that when Lucretia Mott was denied the right to serve as a delegate to the World Anti-Slavery Convention because she was a women, she joined Elizabeth Cady Stanton in organizing the first women's rights convention in Seneca Falls, New York, in 1848. William Lloyd Garrison was a delegate and supported their demand for women's suffrage.

ASSESSMENT

You can assess students informally during the class discussion. Alternatively, you can ask the groups to submit written responses to the questions.

EXTENSIONS AND MODIFICATIONS

Point out that many of the women involved in reform were middle-class or wealthy white women. Lead a discussion of how working-class white women and African-American women would have reacted to abolitionism and women's rights. What barriers would they have faced in trying to become involved in those movements?

What Have Women to Do with Slavery? A Dialogue

AN ARTICLE FROM *THE LIBERATOR*, NOVEMBER 1, 1839

Mrs. A. Is it possible, my dear Harriet, that what I have heard is true, and that you have actually joined the Anti-Slavery Society?

Harriet. It is so, aunt; I became satisfied that it was my duty.

Mrs. A. I thought your mother did not approve of your engaging in this matter.

Harriet. She did not, but then she wished me to act according to my own sense of right; she says I am of an age to decide for myself upon questions of right and wrong.

Mrs. A. I am sorry that my sister has been so weakly indulgent to you; I doubt not that in a short time I shall hear that she also has turned abolitionist, and if your uncle does not prevent his name from being so disgraced, she will sign the petitions of Congress with other misguided women.

Harriet. Excuse me, dear aunt, but I cannot help hoping that your fears may be realized. But why is it that you are displeased with what I have done? I thought you told me that you were convinced that slavery is sinful; and you have often said that you felt as much for the poor slaves as I do.

Mrs. A. And I dare say I do; but I do not approve of the doings of the abolitionists in the first place; and most of all do I disapprove of women's meddling with such things.

*The underlining is used for the activity on p. 100.

Harriet. Why so?

Mrs. A. It is evident, my dear, that men are appointed by Providence to make and administer the laws; it is a violation of the Divine Order when women interfere in politics. Slavery is the law of the land—it is a political question—and therefore there is a great impropriety in women's meddling with the subject.

Harriet. Waiving the question altogether of the propriety of women having anything to do with politics, is not the subject of slavery in fact a religious and moral question? Its pernicious effects extend to the remotest parts of our country; its poison has entered into the very fibre and muscle, if I may so speak, of our otherwise happy land; <u>not a living soul but directly or indirectly feels its baneful influence, whether they know and confess it, or not.</u>

Mrs. A. Suppose, Harriet, that this extravagant statement of yours were correct—still, what can women do about it? What, for instance, can an ignorant girl like you do? Mr. A., who has studied the subject faithfully, says that he thinks nothing can be done, especially by northerners, and most especially by women. Doubtless, in the course of Providence, slavery, like many other evils that have passed away, will die out; but what, Harriet, can all these silly women do about it?

Harriet. Much, I think, may be done, even by foolish women, to take the worst aspect of the case, though I do not confess to their folly.

Mrs. A. Well, Harriet, that is a specimen of your love of opposition. What good can a foolish woman do for any cause?

Harriet. Why, dear aunt, I have more faith in the intrinsic strength of a good principle than of an evil one; and as I see so many foolish men supporting slavery, which is all evil, by their opinions and practice, I do not see why foolish women, with the strength and the enlightening power of truth on their side, may not do something to overthrow it. But <u>there are some women of good sense and powerful talents in the anti-slavery ranks</u>. I need not name them.

Mrs. A. These are the very women that I blame; they not only depart from the plain path of duty pointed out by Providence themselves, but they mislead others.

Harriet. I cannot think that when we all stand before the bar of Divine Justice, any woman will be condemned for having labored to abolish the greatest and most far-spreading system of wickedness that is to be found in the whole history of man. I find in the New Testament no limits but possibility to the duties of any human being; it seems to me that we are all bound to do "what we can."

Mrs. A. But suppose, for argument's sake, I grant this. What can women do? Nothing, absolutely nothing; they are, most of them, ignorant and impotent.

Harriet. Let them inform themselves in the first place, and that source of weakness will cease; let them study the laws, the history of slavery in their native land; let them know what it really is.

Mrs. A. No woman of a nice sensibility, or of a truly refined delicacy, can bear to read the annals of slavery. I just opened Paxton's letters, and it made me sick for the whole day; it is just so with "Slavery as it is," by Mr. and Mrs. Weld [Angelina Grimké and Theodore Weld]; I took it up in your parlor the other day, and I could not bear to read two pages of it, it made me so unhappy.

Harriet. And yet that book is made up of well authenticated facts, many of them from slaveholders themselves; and what must the poor being have to endure, whose misery is so great we cannot even bear to read of it?

Mrs. A. But, my dear Harriet, what is the use of my making myself so unhappy about them? Of what use are my tears and sighs to the poor creatures?

Harriet. I cannot allow, aunt, that this is all you can do for them, but suppose it were. Put yourself in the place of the oppressed, broken-hearted slave-mother, who, perhaps, has just seen her child sold, to go she knows not whither; would it not be some comfort to her, even if you could not help her, to know that there was one human heart that ached for her sorrows, and that would help her if it could? Are we not bound to give them our tears, our pity, if we can give no more; may not our prayers meet and unite with theirs in fervent supplication to the Father of mercies that he would set them free? But we can, O I am sure we can, every woman can, do much.

Mrs. A. I fear not. Your uncle says you only do harm by all these petitions, for instance.

Harriet. We think otherwise, and while we do, we must still send up petitions; if Congress takes the part of the unjust judge, we must imitate that of the importunate widow; but there are other and perhaps more effectual means in the hands of women.

Mrs. A. What are they, Harriet; I hope it is not speaking in public?

Harriet. I would have those who have the gift, and [feel] so impelled, speak any and every where for these unhappy beings who are cut off from human sympathy. Men will not speak for them; they cannot speak for themselves; shall not the women, even the very children speak for them, if they can? On that God in his wisdom and mercy might inspire them so that the prophet's words might be verified—"Their sons and their daughters shall prophesy." But there is yet another way in which women at the North, and all women who consider slavery sinful, can do something for its abolition.

Mrs. A. And what is that, Harriet?

Harriet. By as far as possible washing their own hands and cleansing their own garments from its foul stain; for all in this land partake of its sin and are born under its condemnation.

Mrs. A. Mercy, Harriet! you speak now like one of the disciples of Garrison; what do you mean? How am I, for instance, under this condemnation? How are my garments or hands stained with the sin of slavery?

Harriet. You live under its laws; you are enriched by its iniquitous gains; your father, husband and sons pay for its support; and what is more horrible than all, they may be obliged, either personally or by proxy, to commit murder to maintain it. The law commands you to give up a fugitive slave, let his master be ever so cruel a tyrant; the slaveholders have an influence in Congress proportioned to the number of their slaves, and then make laws for the free states. The riches of the South are the result of the sighs and groans and bleeding stripes and blistering tears of almost three millions of slaves; and do not northerners share constantly in these riches? What was the original cause of the war in Florida? Slavery. The fugitive slaves found friends and formed connections among the persecuted Indians, and the southerners demanded them and their children as property, and the Indians defended these, men and women as they thought them, in their natural rights, against the christian republicans. This war has already cost the nation more than twenty millions of dollars, and every man in the free states has to pay his tax for it. Should the slaves ever dare to imitate our forefathers simply in the vindication of their claims to humanity, your sons may be called upon to go and help murder them for it. This statement, dear aunt, I believe no one contradicts. Does not slavery, then, touch us all, every one of us? Have not northern mothers and wives and sisters something to do with slavery?

Mrs. A. It makes me perfectly nervous to hear you talk so, Harriet, and what is the use of it? I again ask, what can women do to abolish slavery, even if it were safe to do it, though your uncle says it is not?

Harriet. They can do much: they can petition Congress against its continuance in the District of Columbia and the Territories; they can protest against it every where and upon all fitting occasions; they can teach their sons and daughters, as soon as they can understand them, how sinful it is; they can urge upon them the duty of making every effort for its abolition. Northern women can refuse to marry slaveholders; northern mothers can ask their consciences whether they could stand before God guiltless if they had acquiesced in the marriage of their daughters with slaveholders.

Mrs. A. But, my dear Harriet, some slaveholders are very good men: and suppose two young people were strongly attached to each other, must a girl in such a case refuse to marry a man she really loves?

Harriet. I think so; if she views slavery as it really is, she could never become a slaveholder herself, as she would by such a union. Neither do I think a christian woman would long continue to love a man who could keep slaves after he knew how great a sin it was.

Mrs. A. Perhaps he cannot be convinced it is a sin; perhaps he thinks it right, and the best thing for the slaves.

Harriet. It is her duty to try to convince him in every way in her power, and if she fail in this, to give him the strongest testimony she can of the strength of her own conviction, by resigning her love for him for what ought to be always her highest love, a love of right, a love of justice, love of humanity.

Mrs. A. But, if she were to marry him, she might perhaps convert him to her own views, and so she would be the means of redeeming his slaves from bondage.

Harriet. I could not for one day—for one hour, eat bread earned for me by slaves. I should feel degraded in my own eyes; the poor negro by whose forced and unrequited labor I am supported would be a higher being than myself in my own estimation; I should be the true slave. But I cannot imagine myself as loving a man who was defrauding human beings of their most precious possession every moment of his life; to be his wife would be to live under the most odious, the most abject of all bondage, that of my moral nature.

Mrs. A. Oh Harriet! to accuse slaveholders of fraud is not fair. You know that most of the present southern slaveholders have inherited their slaves, or they have purchased those who are already in bondage, and have been inherited by their owners.

Harriet. There is no time, no circumstances, no changing of hands, that can ever justify theft or fraud; a slave is a man defrauded of his natural, his dearest, his inalienable rights; and whoever holds him as such stands convicted of being in fact accessory to an act of the most daring and cruel robbery.

Mrs. A. Then, Harriet, you will not marry the rich Mr.————————, who is so much in love with you?

Harriet. No, never, while by these hands I can minister to my necessities; better and happier would it be to be a beggar in the streets, a sordid dependant on a grudging charity, than with my views be the wife of a rich slaveholder.

E. L. F. [possibly Eliza Lee Follen, a prominent Bostonian abolitionist]

Source: Old Sturbridge Village, *The Liberator,* November 1, 1839; available at http://www.osv.org/school/lesson_plans/ShowLessons.php?PageID=P&LessonID=36&DocID=131&UnitID=/.

QUESTIONS:

1. To analyze a document, historians must have a broad understanding of the historical context of the period. Use your textbook and the underlined phrases in the dialog to summarize the broader political context of the period. Set the document in the context of antebellum reform and the growing sectional divide over slavery.

2. How would you characterize the aunt? What are her views on women and on abolition?

3. How would you characterize Harriet? What are her views on women and on abolition?

4. What social constraints on women can you infer from the text?

5. According to the article, on what grounds were women to oppose slavery? Which of the forces behind reform discussed at the beginning of the lesson can you find in the dialog?

6. What measures were women to take to oppose slavery? By implication, what actions were they not to engage in? Does the author see a difference in how men and women should oppose slavery?

7. What does the author see as women's appropriate role in politics?

8. William Lloyd Garrison was the editor of *The Liberator*. What do you think his views on women's rights might have been?

Copyright ©2009 by International Debate Education Association
The Publisher grants permission for the reproduction of this worksheet except for commercial purposes. Activity sheets may be downloaded from www.idebate.org/handouts.htm

9. The Lincoln–Douglas Debates

INSTRUCTIONAL OBJECTIVES
Students will be able to:
- Explain the sectional tensions leading up to the Civil War
- Analyze the Democratic and Republican positions on the extension of slavery
- Evaluate the importance of slavery as a cause of the conflict

DESCRIPTION

Students will use the Lincoln–Douglas debates to explore the growing significance of sectionalism and the issue of slavery and its expansion in the years leading to the Civil War. In groups, they will prepare to present the key points of each debate and discuss their meaning and implications.

TIME

120 minutes (can be presented in one block or in two regular class periods)

MATERIALS

Full transcripts of the seven Lincoln–Douglas Debates found at http://www.nps.gov/liho/historyculture/debates.htm. (You will need enough copies of each debate so that each member of the group analyzing the debate has a copy.)
Analyzing Lincoln–Douglas (copies for each student)

CLASS LAYOUT AND GROUPING OF STUDENTS

The class will work in small groups before presenting their findings in a full class discussion.

PROCEDURE

1. Explain that the 1858 Lincoln–Douglas debates were a series of political debates between Abraham Lincoln, the Republican candidate for the U.S. Senate from Illinois, and Stephen A. Douglas, the Democratic candidate. There were seven debates, and they all centered on the issue of slavery and its ramifications. Tell the class that they will analyze the debates to help them understand the issue of slavery in the context of the politics of the period.

2. Review the historical context of the debates, emphasizing the following:
   - Compromise of 1850
   - Fugitive slave laws

- Kansas-Nebraska Act
- "Bleeding Kansas"—Admission of Kansas under Lecompton constitution
- Dred Scott decision
- Popular sovereignty

3. Set the stage for the debates, contrasting the two men: Lincoln was a relative unknown, while Douglas was a sitting senator and national leader of the Democratic Party. Lincoln was six feet four inches, Douglas five feet four inches. Lincoln spoke slowly, Douglas rapidly. Lincoln, who attacked "the Slave Power," was born in the southern state of Kentucky. Douglas, who hoped his principle of "popular sovereignty" would find support in the South, was born in the free state of Vermont.

4. Explain that the students will break into seven groups, and that each group will analyze one debate in preparation for presenting a five- to seven-minute overview to the rest of the class. Half of each group should read and synthesize Lincoln's speech, while the other half synthesizes Douglas's. Answer any questions and then have students count off by sevens. Have students with the same numbers assemble into groups.

5. Distribute Analyzing Lincoln–Douglas and the appropriate debate transcript packets to each group. Tell the students that they can use the activity sheet to help them summarize their candidate's stand on the issues. Explain that not every debate covered all issues, and that intermingled with a discussion of principles was a lot of petty political bickering. Remind the students that although half of each group is studying one speech, the group as a whole is responsible for presenting an overview of the entire speech, so members must work together to prepare their presentation.

6. After the groups have finished their research, call for the groups' attention and ask each group to present its findings. The groups should present in the order the debates were held:
   - Ottawa
   - Freeport
   - Jonesboro
   - Charleston
   - Galesburg
   - Quincy
   - Alton

   After each group presents, reiterate the key messages of that debate and explain any that the students may not have recognized. Note the importance of the Freeport Doctrine and what it meant for Douglas's relationship with Southern Democrats and his hopes for the presidency. Continue until all groups have finished.

7. After all debates have been presented, hold a general discussion about the debates' content. Conclude by noting that while Lincoln lost the election, this series of speeches drew audiences from across the Midwest and his name became well-known—so much so that he ran for and won the U.S. presidential race two years later in 1860.

Assessment

You can informally assess each group as it presents its findings.

Extensions and modifications

Download or direct students to http://www.knox.edu/debates.xml to listen to the podcast series, one podcast for each debate plus a summary. While Lincoln and Douglas debated over many months for hours at a time, the podcasts provide background on the issues, the content, and even the strategies of Lincoln and Douglas in less than 10 minutes per podcast. Rodney Davis and Douglas Wilson, directors of the Lincoln Studies Center at Knox College in Illinois, narrate the podcasts with descriptions of the crowds, the weather, and even the modes of transportation the people used to attend the debates.

Analyzing Lincoln–Douglas

Location of Debate: _____

	Lincoln	Douglas
Dred Scott		
Kansas-Nebraska Act		
Fugitive slave laws		
Slavery in the territories/ admission of states		
States' rights		
Equality of races		

Copyright ©2009 by International Debate Education Association
The Publisher grants permission for the reproduction of this worksheet except for commercial purposes.
Activity sheets may be downloaded from www.idebate.org/handouts.htm

10. Reconstruction

INSTRUCTIONAL OBJECTIVES

Students will be able to:

* Contrast the Reconstruction plans of Lincoln, the moderates, and Radical Republicans
* Evaluate the ideas underlying these competing Reconstruction plans

DESCRIPTION

Students will assemble in a session of Congress to debate plans for Reconstruction.

TIME

60 minutes

MATERIALS

Plans for Reconstruction (copy for each student)

CLASS LAYOUT AND GROUPING OF STUDENTS

Students will analyze the primary material in their usual seating arrangements. For the Congress, desks should be organized in a circle or in another arrangement that will facilitate debate.

PROCEDURE

1. Tell the class that it will convene as the U.S. House of Representatives to debate the future of the South following the end of the Civil War.

2. Set the scene for the debate. Explain that the Civil War decimated the South. Cities such as Atlanta and Richmond were in ruins, and the region's farm equipment, livestock, factories, and infrastructure had been destroyed. The South, never as prosperous as the North, was desperately poor. Over 250,000—one-fourth of the white male population of military age—had lost their lives. Former slaves had few resources, and the Black Codes restricted their freedom. The North, too, suffered. Approximately 360,000 Union troops were lost, and the North learned of the atrocities at Andersonville, in which almost 13,000 Union prisoners died of malnutrition, exposure, and disease.

3. Explain that the debate over Reconstruction centered around three issues:
   - Under what terms were the former Confederate States to be readmitted to the Union, and who should establish those terms—Congress or the President?
   - Who should be punished for the rebellion and how?
   - What was to be done, if anything, to aid the newly freed slaves?

   Tell the class that the nation was deeply divided over these questions, with moderates favoring lenient policies toward the South, and Radicals wanting a harsh plan to punish the region and to ensure total equality of blacks.

4. Distribute Views on Reconstruction, and ask the students to read the material in preparation for convening Congress. Give the class 15 minutes to read the selections, then ask them what the key elements of the moderate and radical positions were. Emphasize the following:

Moderate	Radical
View toward South: Rebel states, though insurrectionist, had never left the Union because the Constitution did not grant the right of secession.	**View toward South:** States in rebellion were outside the Union, and therefore could be treated as conquered territory to be dealt with as the conqueror saw fit.
Terms of Reconstruction: • Pardon for most Southerners who had not held high office, once they swore loyalty to the Constitution and to the Union • States readmitted once 10 percent of the voting population had taken the oath. • No plan for former slaves, *or* belief that the states, not the federal government, should set policy for freedmen	**Terms of Reconstruction:** • Military rule • Enfranchising emancipated blacks • Severe punishment of Confederate leaders • Assertion of Congressional supremacy in assessing how the South should be restored

5. Arrange the seats in a circle and convene the Congress. Tell the students that this session is to develop a plan for Reconstruction. The Congress can adopt either the moderate or radical plan, or develop a different plan. Make sure that during the debate the "representatives" defend the positions they are taking.

ASSESSMENT

You will be able to assess the students' understanding of the debate over Reconstruction during the session of Congress.

EXTENSIONS AND MODIFICATIONS

- Organize a debate about whether or not Reconstruction achieved its goals.
- Debate the following: Radical Reconstruction ultimately made life more difficult for African Americans in the South.

Plans for Reconstruction

LINCOLN AND THE MODERATES

ABRAHAM LINCOLN ON RECONSTRUCTION

With malice toward none, with charity for all, with firmness in the right as God gives us to see the right, let us strive on to finish the work we are in, to bind up the nation's wounds, to care for him who shall have borne the battle and for his widow and his orphan, to do all which may achieve and cherish a just and lasting peace among ourselves and with all nations.

Second Inaugural Address, March 4, 1865

Source: National Center, http://www.nationalcenter.org/LincolnSecondInaugural. html.

LINCOLN'S PLAN

I, Abraham Lincoln . . . do proclaim, declare, and make known to all persons who have, directly or by implication, participated in the existing rebellion, except as hereinafter excepted, that a full pardon is hereby granted to them and each of them with restoration of all rights of property, except as to slaves . . . upon the condition that every such person shall take . . . an oath, and thenceforward keep and maintain such oath inviolate. . . .

The persons exempted from the benefits of the foregoing provisions are [high Confederate officials, U.S. military officers who resigned their commissions and aided the rebellion, and those guilty of crimes against prisoners of war].

And I do further proclaim, declare, and make known that whenever, in any of the States of Arkansas, Texas, Louisiana, Mississippi, Tennessee, Alabama, Georgia, Florida, South Carolina, and North Carolina, a number of persons, not less than one-tenth in number of the votes cast in such State at the presidential election of the year of our Lord [1860], each having taken the oath aforesaid . . . shall reestablish a State Government which . . . shall be recognized as the true government of the State. . . .

Abraham Lincoln, Proclamation, December 8, 1863

Source: Bernard Feder, *Viewpoints USA* (American Book Company, 1967), pp. 162–163.

HENRY J. RAYMOND, MODERATE REPRESENTATIVE FROM NEW YORK, FORMER EDITOR AND OWNER OF THE *NEW YORK TIMES*, AND SUPPORTER OF LINCOLN

Mr. Chairman, I am here to act with those who seek to complete the restoration of the Union. . . . We have great communities of men, permanent interests of great States, to deal with, and we are bound to deal with them in a large and liberal spirit. It may be for the welfare of this nation that we shall cherish toward the millions of our people lately in rebellion feelings of hatred and distrust; that we shall nurse the bitterness that their infamous treason has naturally and justly engendered, and make that the basis of our future dealings with them. Possibly we may best teach them the lessons of liberty, by visiting upon them the worst excesses of despotism. Possibly they may best learn to practice justice toward others, to admire and emulate our republican institutions, by suffering at our hands the absolute rule we denounce in others. It may be best for us and for them that we discard, in all our dealings with them, all the obligations and requirements of the Constitution, and assert as the only law for them the unrestrained will of conquerors and masters.

I confess I do not sympathize with the sentiments or the opinions which would dictate such a course. I would exact of them all needed and all just guarantees for their future loyalty to the Constitution and laws of the United States. I would exact from them, or impose upon them through the constitutional legislation of Congress, and by enlarging and extending, if necessary, the scope and powers of the Freedmen's Bureau, proper care and protection for the helpless and friendless freedmen, so lately their slaves. I would exercise a rigid scrutiny into the character and loyalty of the men whom they may send to Congress, before I allowed them to participate in the high prerogative of legislating for the nation. But I would seek to allay rather than stimulate the animosities and hatred, however just they may be, to which the war has given rise. But for our own sake as well as for theirs I would not visit upon them a policy of confiscation which has been discarded in the policy and practical conduct of every civilized nation on the face of the globe.

I believe it important for us as well as for them that we should cultivate friendly relations with them, that we should seek the promotion of their interests as part and parcel of our own. We have been their enemies in war, in peace let us show ourselves their friends. I hope and believe we shall soon see the day when the people of the southern States will show us, by evidences that we cannot mistake, that they have returned, in all sincerity and good faith, to their allegiance to the Union; that they intend to join henceforth with us in promoting its prosperity, in defending the banner of its glory, and in fighting the battles of democratic freedom, not only here, but wherever the issue may be forced upon our acceptance.

Source: Henry J. Raymond, "Speech on Reconstruction," *African-American History Online*. Facts On File, Inc., http://www.fofweb.com/activelink2.asp? ItemID=WE 01&iPin=E02320&SingleRecord=True.

Radical Republican

Representative Thaddeus Stevens of Pennsylvania, leader of the Radical Republicans

We hold it to be the duty of the government to inflict condign punishment on the rebel belligerents, and so weaken their hands that they can never again endanger the Union; and so reform their municipal institutions as to make them republican in spirit as well as in name. . . .

. . . the foundation of their institutions, both political, municipal, and social *must* be broken up and *relaid*, or all our blood and treasure have been spent in vain. This can only be done by treating and holding them as a conquered people. Then all things which we can desire to do follow with logical and legitimate authority. As conquered territory Congress would have full power to legislate for them; for the territories are not under the Constitution except so far as the express power to govern them is given to Congress. They would be held in a territorial condition until they are fit to form State Constitutions, republican in fact not in form only, and ask admission into the Union as new States. If Congress approve of their Constitutions, and think they have done works meet for repentance they would be admitted as new States. If their Constitutions are not approved of, they would be sent back . . . until they shall have learned to venerate the Declaration of Independence.

This war had its origin in treason without one spark of justice. It was prosecuted before notice of it, by robbing our forts and armories, and our navy-yards; by stealing our money from the mints and depositories, and by surrendering our forts and navies by perjurers who had sworn to support the Constitution. In its progress our prisoners, by the authority of their government, were slaughtered in cold blood. . . . Sixty thousand of our prisoners have been deliberately starved to death because they would not enlist in the rebel armies. The graves at Andersonville [notorious Confederate prisoner-of-war camp] have each an accusing tongue. The purpose and avowed object of the enemy "to found an empire whose corner-stone should be slavery," render its perpetuity or revival dangerous to human liberty.

We propose to confiscate all the estate of every rebel belligerent whose estate was worth $10,000 or whose land exceeded two hundred acres in quantity. . . . By thus forfeiting the estates of the leading rebels, the Government would have 394,000,000 of acres. . . . Give if you please forty acres to each adult male freedman. Suppose there are one million of them. That would require 40,000,000 of acres. . . .

The whole fabric of southern society must be changed. . . . How can republican institutions, free schools, free churches, free social intercourse exist in a mingled community of nabobs and serfs; of the owners of twenty thousand acre manors with lordly palaces, and the occupants of narrow huts inhabited by "low white trash?" . . .

The property of the rebels shall pay our national debt, and indemnify freedmen and loyal sufferers.

Source: Thaddeus Stephens, "Speech on Reconstruction," *African-American History Online*. Facts On File, Inc., http://www.fofweb.com/activelink2.asp? ItemID=WE 01&iPin=E02330&SingleRecord=True.

Chapter 4
Challenges of a Modern Nation

Chapter 4 asks students to analyze six key events as the United States emerged as a modern industrial state and faced the Depression and World War II. They explore how nativism, race, and religion impacted immigration and engage in a role-play to understand Populist and Progressive reform. Using primary documents students then analyze the reasons for, and opposition to, U.S. entry into World War I. In the fourth lesson they explore the campaign for women's suffrage. Students then learn about the New Deal and its lasting impact on U.S. government. Finally, they debate Truman's decision to use the atomic bomb.

11. Immigration

INSTRUCTIONAL OBJECTIVES

Students will be able to:
- Assess the challenges, opportunities, and contributions of different immigrant groups
- Understand the impact of nativism, race, and religion on immigration
- Describe key trends in U.S. immigration policy and analyze the forces behind them

DESCRIPTION

Students will work in groups to research the experience of four immigrant groups: Irish in the 1840s, Protestant Germans in 1848, Russian Jews in the 1890s, and Chinese in the 1920s. The students will then engage in historical role-play as they share their experience with members of the other groups.

TIME

60 minutes

MATERIALS

The New Colossus (copy for each student)
Timeline of Immigration Policy (copy for each student)
Our Immigrant Experience (copy for each student)

PREPARATION

Reserve the computer lab.

CLASS LAYOUT AND GROUPING OF STUDENTS

Student will work in specific "immigrant" groups in the computer lab and will reassemble in groups for the role-play and discussion.

PROCEDURE

1. Distribute "The New Colossus." Explain that Emma Lazarus wrote this poem as a donation for an auction to raise money for the construction of the pedestal of the Statue of Liberty. The statue, whose formal name is "Liberty Enlightening the World," was originally given

to the United States by France as a monument to shared republican values; the poem, however, transformed the statue into a symbol of welcome for immigrants.

2. Explain that in this lesson students will debate whether the thoughts in that poem reflect the reality of U.S. immigration.

3. Divide the class into four groups of immigrants: Irish in the 1840s, Protestant Germans in 1848, Russian Jews in the 1890s, and Chinese in the 1920s. Distribute Timeline of Immigration Policy and Our Immigrant Experience. Ask each group to complete the questionnaire and determine whether Lazarus's poem reflects their experience. Alert them that they will be sharing their experience and analysis with other students.

4. Once the students have completed their research, reorganize the class into groups of four that include representatives from each of the ethnic groups. Ask the students to share their immigrant experience with other members of the group. Circulate as the groups engage in discussion to ensure they are on topic and to respond to any concerns or questions.

5. Wrap up the discussion by calling for the class's attention and asking the students as a whole to discuss and assess Lazarus's ideas in light of their findings.

ASSESSMENT

You can informally assess students as they present their immigrant experience to the integrated groups. Alternatively, you can ask the immigrant groups to submit their findings for evaluation.

EXTENSIONS AND MODIFICATIONS

Debate the following: Race and religion have always mattered in America's response to immigration.

The New Colossus

Not like the brazen giant of Greek fame,

With conquering limbs astride from land to land;

Here at our sea-washed, sunset gates shall stand

A mighty woman with a torch, whose flame

Is the imprisoned lightning, and her name

Mother of Exiles. From her beacon-hand

Glows world-wide welcome; her mild eyes command

The air-bridged harbor that twin cities frame.

"Keep ancient lands, your storied pomp!" cries she

With silent lips. "Give me your tired, your poor,

Your huddled masses yearning to breathe free,

The wretched refuse of your teeming shore.

Send these, the homeless, tempest-tost to me,

I lift my lamp beside the golden door!"

Emma Lazarus

Source: http://www.libertystatepark.com/emma.htm

Timeline of U.S. Immigration Policy

1790 Federal government establishes a two-year residency requirement for citizenship.

1875 First exclusionary act bars convicts, prostitutes, and Chinese contract laborers from entry into the United States.

1882 In the first significant restriction on free immigration in U.S. history, the Chinese Exclusion Act excludes Chinese laborers from entry for 10 years. Chinese non-laborers wishing to immigrate must obtain a certificate from the Chinese government.

1885 Contract laborers' entry barred.

1891 Paupers, polygamists, and persons with contagious diseases are excluded from entry to the United States.

1903 Additional categories of persons excluded, including anarchists.

1904 Congress indefinitely extends the provisions of the Chinese Exclusion Act.

1907 Additional categories of persons excluded, including the feeble-minded, those with tuberculosis, persons with physical or mental defects, and persons under age 16 without parents.

1907 "Gentleman's agreement" between United States and Japan curtails Japanese immigration.

1917 All Asians banned from entry. Literacy test introduced.

1921 Quota Act sets an annual immigration ceiling at 350,000, and establishes a new nationality quota designed to restrict immigration from eastern and southern Europe.

1924 National Origins Act reduces the annual immigration ceiling to 165,000. A revised quota reduces admissions to 2 percent of each nationality group's representation in the 1890 census.

1927 Immigration Ceiling reduced to 150,000; the quota is revised to 2 percent of each nationality's representation in the 1920 census. This basic law remains in effect through 1965.

1929 National Origins Act. The annual immigration ceiling of 150,000 is made permanent, with 70 percent of admissions slated for those coming from Northern and Western Europe, with the other 30 percent reserved for those coming from Southern and Eastern Europe.

1948 Displaced Persons Act permits entry for 400,000 persons displaced by World War II, provided refugees can pass security check.

1952 McCarran-Walter Act removes race as a basis for exclusion. Denies entry based on political ideology (e.g., if they are Communists or former Nazis).

1965 Nationality quotas are abolished. Annual ceiling of 170,000 established for immigration from the Eastern Hemisphere, 120,000 ceiling placed on immigration from the Western Hemisphere.

1978 Worldwide immigration ceiling of 290,000 replaces the separate ceilings.

1986 Immigration Reform and Control Act raises annual ceiling to 540,000. Amnesty offered to illegal aliens who can prove continuous residence in the United States since January 1.

1990 Immigration Act of 1990. The annual immigration ceiling is further raised to 700,000 for 1992, 1993, and 1994; thereafter, the ceiling will drop to 675,000 a year. Ten thousand permanent resident visas are offered to those immigrants agreeing to invest at least $1 million in U.S. urban areas or $500,000 in U.S. rural areas. People can no longer be denied admittance based on their beliefs, statements, or associations.

1996 Immigration Act attempts to curb illegal immigration by doubling the U.S. Border Patrol and mandating the construction of fences at the most heavily trafficked areas of the U.S.–Mexico border.

1996 Illegal immigrants become ineligible for virtually all federal and state benefits except emergency medical care, immunization programs, and disaster relief.

Adapted from PBS, *New Americans,* http://www.pbs.org/independentlens/ newamericans/foreducators_lesson_plan_03.html.

Copyright ©2009 by International Debate Education Association
The Publisher grants permission for the reproduction of this worksheet except for commercial purposes. Activity sheets may be downloaded from www.idebate.org/handouts.htm

Our Immigrant Experience

Instructions: Use Timeline of Immigration Policy and the Internet to answer the following questions about your immigrant group. Be prepared to share your findings with other members of the class and to explain why Emma Lazarus's poem does or does not reflect the reality of your group's experience.

Immigrant Group:_____

1. Why did the group come to the United States?

2. Were there legal barriers to entry? If so, explain. Why were the restrictions established?

3. What kind of reception did your group receive? How did Americans view the coming of your group? In researching this question, remember to search on "nativism" (anti-immigrant sentiment).

4. Were there any periods in American history when your group might have received a different reception? Why?

5. Was America the "golden door" for your group? How did your group fare in America?

6. Review American immigration policy and be prepared to summarize its trends. How would your group have fared under current regulations?

For an overview of immigration, see The Ellis Island-Statue of Liberty Foundation, *The Peopling of America,* http://www.ellisisland.org/immexp/wseix_4_3.asp?

For a more in-depth history of the response to immigration, see Roger Daniels, "The Triumph of Nativism," http://www.hsp.org/files/comingtoamericareading.pdf.

Copyright ©2009 by International Debate Education Association
The Publisher grants permission for the reproduction of this worksheet except for commercial purposes. Activity sheets may be downloaded from www.idebate.org/handouts.htm

12. Turn of the 20th Century Reform

INSTRUCTIONAL OBJECTIVES

Students will be able to:
- Understand the lives experienced by Americans of various social, ethnic, and economic groups at the turn of the 20th century
- Understand the key issues facing the nation
- Understand Populism and Progressivism, their limitations, and alternatives offered by other groups
- Analyze the concerns of competing groups
- Present an overview of reform during this period

DESCRIPTION

Students will role-play individuals from turn of the 20th century America, using what they have learned to describe life during this period. They will present the problems and issues of concern to their character and analyze solutions to these problems.

TIME

One week for research (homework assignment); 60-minute class period

MATERIALS

Characters
Life and Issues (copy for each student)

PREPARATION

Prepare the list of characters. You may use the suggested list below or adapt the list to the needs of the class. The characters involved should reflect key elements and experiences from American at the turn of the 20th century.

Cut the list of characters into strips and put them into an envelope or open box.

CLASS LAYOUT AND GROUPING OF STUDENTS

Students will remain in their usual seating arrangement for the discussion.

PROCEDURE

Part 1: Research

1. Explain that the students will extend their knowledge of the United States at the turn of the 20th century by role-playing characters from that era. Some will be historical figures, and some will be representatives of key groups. Students are to research their character and come to class prepared to describe what life was like for that character. They will also present a summary of the problems and issues that were important to that individual, as well as possible solutions to those problems that individual would have recommended. Finally, students are to determine whether or not society accepted those solutions.

2. Distribute Life and Issues and review the assignment.

3. Circulate around the class, asking students to take a character at random from the envelope or box. Note who has each character and keep the sheet for reference during the discussion.

4. Tell the class that they have a week to prepare their characters.

Part II: Discussion

1. Ask the students to assume their characters in preparation for a discussion of the issues facing the United States at the turn of the 20th century. Remind them that they must stay in character throughout the discussion.

2. Ask the class to set the stage. What was America like at the turn of the century? What would the everyday life of their character have been like? Students should become aware of the dramatic differences in American society during this period.

3. Ask a student to name the issue their character would think highly important, and how their character might address it. Ask the other members of the class if their characters would have agreed, and how they might have reacted to the proposed solution. Note the basic issue and the suggested solutions on the board. Continue choosing students to name issues, using your assignment sheet to ensure that characters representing all basic issues—women and minority rights, economic consolidation, labor, and so on—are covered

4. Ask the students how American government and society addressed the problem—or whether it did

5. Conclude the discussion by asking the class if they see any parallels between turn of the 20th century America and contemporary America.

ASSESSMENT

You can assess the students informally during the discussion. Alternatively, you can ask the students to submit written reports on their characters for evaluation.

EXTENSIONS AND MODIFICATIONS

Remind the students that this period was one of great economic disparity between the very rich and the average American. Debate whether such disparity is good for a democracy.

Characters

Alice Paul

Alva Vanderbilt

Andrew Carnegie

Booker T. Washington

Child worker in textile mill

Chinese laborer in California

Cuban cigar maker

Eleanor Roosevelt

Eugene V. Debs

Henry Cabot Lodge

Hispanic ranch hand in New Mexico

Ida B. Wells

J.P. Morgan

Jane Addams

Japanese laborer on Hawaiian plantation

Jewish garment worker living on New York's Lower East Side

John D. Rockefeller

Kansas farmer

Lincoln Steffens

Mississippi sharecropper

Newspaper boy

Pittsburgh steelworker

Pullman car worker

Sioux Indian

Student at Vassar College

Upton Sinclair

W.E.B. DuBois

William Gladden

Copyright ©2009 by International Debate Education Association
The Publisher grants permission for the reproduction of this worksheet except for commercial purposes.
Activity sheets may be downloaded from www.idebate.org/handouts.htm

Life and Issues

Instructions: Research your assigned character and be prepared to describe the kind of life that individual had at the turn of the 20th century. If you are researching a specific individual, make sure that your analysis goes beyond the events of the person's life to describe what that person's general experience was like—for example, as a middle-class, educated woman or a wealthy industrialist. Determine what problems and issues would have been of concern to that individual, and what solutions he or she might have advocated.

Assigned character:_____

Life experience:

Problems of concern:

Possible solutions:

Did the United States adopt these solutions? Be specific.

Copyright ©2009 by International Debate Education Association
The Publisher grants permission for the reproduction of this worksheet except for commercial purposes.
Activity sheets may be downloaded from www.idebate.org/handouts.htm

13. World War I

INSTRUCTIONAL OBJECTIVES

Students will be able to:

- Understand the events leading to U.S. entry into World War I
- Evaluate Woodrow Wilson's reasons for going to war
- Understand the reasons behind opposition to entry

DESCRIPTION

Students will work in small groups to analyze primary documents to understand the reasons for, and opposition to, U.S. entry into World War I.

TIME

60 minutes

MATERIALS

Events Leading to U.S. Entry into World War I (copy for each student)
Wilson's War Message, April 2, 1917 (copy for each student)
Opposition to Wilson's War Message (copy for each student)
Alternate Realities (copy for each student)

CLASS LAYOUT AND GROUPING OF STUDENTS

Students will work in small groups for the first part of the lesson, then resume their usual seating arrangements for the discussion.

PROCEDURE

1. Explain that in August 1914 European nations became embroiled in a devastating war that the United States wanted to stay out of. Tell the students that in this lesson they will review the events that eventually drew America into that war in 1917.

2. Explain that shortly after the war began, the United States declared its neutrality. Review the factors behind that decision, emphasizing:
   - Ethnic divisions in America
   - Wilson's suspicions about the war aims of Britain and France
   - America's historical isolation from European embroilments

- U.S. geographical remoteness from the fighting
- Tangled and confusing causes of war among the imperial powers
- Use of war was at odds with the period's Progressive spirit, which contended that human beings were reasonable and capable of settling disputes peacefully

3. Distribute Events Leading to U.S. Entry into World War I, and review.

4. Distribute Wilson's War Message, April 2, 1917, Opposition to Wilson's War Message, and Alternate Realities. Organize the class into groups of four to six and tell the groups to analyze the documents to determine:
   - Wilson's reasons for going to war
   - Opponents' perceptions of why the nation was going to war
   - Opponents' reasons for opposing war
   - Alternate policies

5. Once the groups have completed the assignment, return the class to their regular seating arrangement. Have the groups report on Wilson's reasons for going to war and what his opponents saw as the real reasons. Why did his opponents not want the United States to become involved? Note these on the board and ask the class to evaluate the reasons.

6. Ask the class to summarize alternative policies. Note them on the board and lead a discussion about whether they were realistic.

7. When presenting Wilson's reasons for entering the war, the class will undoubtedly emphasize German submarine warfare. Make sure that they also note Wilson's desire to make the world "safe for democracy." Ask the class why they think Wilson included this? Given the situation in Europe, was this a realistic goal? What does this goal say about Wilson?

8. Conclude by summarizing the impact that U.S. entry had on the war.

Assessment
You can informally assess the students as they present their findings and during the class discussion.

Extensions and modifications
Ask the class to study the experience of dissenters during the war. Then, debate the assertion: Wilson wanted to make the world safe for democracy, but not in the United States.
Debate whether it is ever valid to go to war to protect or extend democracy.

Events Leading to U.S. Entry into World War I

1914   August 1: Outbreak of World War I, pitting Germany and Austria-Hungary against Britain, France, and Russia.

August 4: Wilson issues neutrality proclamation.

August 15: U.S. government announces that "loans by American bankers to any foreign nation which is at war are inconsistent with the true spirit of neutrality."

November 4: Great Britain announces that the waters of the North Sea are a war zone and begins mining the area.

December: Wilson sends his personal adviser, Edward M. House, to propose American mediation in the conflict. Months of discussions with the belligerents end inconclusively, with House cabling, "Everybody seems to want peace but nobody is willing to concede enough to get it."

December 23: Britain revives the doctrine of the continuous voyage to intercept neutral ships going to Germany and to nations bordering the Baltic Sea under the control of the Germans.

1915   February 4: Germany announces that the waters around the British Isles are a war zone and that enemy merchant ships will be destroyed on sight without provision for the safety of passengers and crew. The German government also warns that neutral craft that enter the war zone do so at their own risk.

February 10: The U.S. government calls German policy "an indefensible violation of neutral rights," and warns that it will hold Germany strictly answerable for the loss of American vessels or lives.

March 11: The British proclaim a blockade of all German ports, with all merchant vessels going to or from them liable to seizure and confiscation.

March 28: American citizen dies in sinking of the British passenger ship *Falaba*.

May 1: During a fight between a German submarine and British naval patrol, the American tanker *Gulflight* is struck by a torpedo, causing the loss of two Americans.

May 1: The Germany embassy in Washington warns that Americans entering the war zone around Great Britain do so at their own risk.

May 7: A German submarine sinks the British transatlantic steamer *Lusitania* without warning off the Irish coast. Nearly 1,200 lives are lost, including those of 128 Americans.

May 13: The United States demands that Germany abandon unrestricted submarine warfare, disavow the sinking of the *Lusitania*, and make reparations for the loss of U.S. lives.

August 19: Two Americans die in the sinking of the British steamer *Arabic* off Ireland.

September 1: The German ambassador to the United States offers the *Arabic* pledge, promising that liners will not be sunk without warning or provision for the safety of the passengers, provided the liners do not try to escape or offer resistance.

September: Wilson reluctantly agrees to float general loans to belligerents.

October 5: Germany apologizes and offers indemnity for the loss of lives on the *Arabic*.

November 21: Germany secretly authorizes submarine commanders to sink all ships plying the English Channel.

1916   January 27: Wilson launches nationwide whistle-stop campaign to generate support for preparedness.

February 8: German declaration that all armed enemy merchant vessels would be sunk without warning raises fears in Congress of further U.S.

losses and requests that Wilson warn Americans not to travel on armed vessels.

February 22: Discussions between Wilson's personal adviser Edward House and British Foreign Secretary Edward Grey produce what is known as the House-Grey Memorandum, stipulating that Wilson will call a peace conference when Britain and France deem it appropriate. If Germany refuses to accept the invitation, the United States would probably enter the war against Germany. If Germany accepts, Wilson will help the Allies negotiate a favorable peace. Neither the Allies nor the Central Powers desire a peace conference.

March 23: A German submarine sinks the French cross-channel passenger ship *Sussex*, resulting in injury to several Americans.

April 18: Wilson issues Germany an ultimatum: the United States will sever relations unless Germany immediately abandons its submarine warfare policy.

May 4: In the Sussex Pledge, Germany agrees to U.S. demands on the condition that the United States compel the Allies to respect the "rules of international law." Wilson accepts the pledge but not the condition.

June 3: The National Defense Act authorizes five-year expansion of the U.S. Army.

October 15: Germany resumes U-boat attacks under search-and-destroy rules.

November 7: Wilson wins reelection on the platform "He Kept Us Out of War."

December 18: In the Peace Note, Wilson requests a statement of war objectives from the belligerents.

1917   January 10: In response to Wilson's December request, the Allies state peace terms—clearly unacceptable to Germany. Germany refuses to state its aims.

January 22: Wilson delivers "Peace without Victory" speech outlining his own program for a peace settlement.

January 31: In a desperate move to end the two-and-a half-year military stalemate in Europe, Germany announces resumption of unrestricted submarine warfare.

February 3: The United States severs relations with Germany.

February 24: The United States receives a copy of the Zimmermann Note sent from the German foreign secretary to the German minister in Mexico stating that if war broke out between Germany and the United States, the minister was to propose an alliance between Germany and Mexico.

February 26: Wilson requests authority from Congress to arm U.S. merchant ships.

March 4: The House overwhelmingly passes the Armed Ship Bill; led by Sen. Robert M. La Follette, antiwar senators—a "little group of willful men" (as Wilson characterized them)—successfully filibuster the bill.

March 12: By executive order, Wilson announces the arming of merchant ships sailing in war zones.

March 13: The Navy Department issues instructions authorizing merchant ships in war zones to take action against submarines.

March 20: Wilson's Cabinet votes unanimously for war.

April: By April 1917, U.S. investors have purchased $2.3 billion in bonds from the Allies in contrast with only about $20 million in German bonds.

April 6: United States declares war on Germany.

Copyright ©2009 by International Debate Education Association
The Publisher grants permission for the reproduction of this worksheet except for commercial purposes. Activity sheets may be downloaded from www.idebate.org/handouts.htm

Wilson's War Message, April 2, 1917

. . . The new [German submarine warfare] policy has swept every restriction aside. Vessels of every kind, whatever their flag, their character, their cargo, their destination, their errand, have been ruthlessly sent to the bottom without warning and without thought of help or mercy for those on board, the vessels of friendly neutrals along with those of belligerents.

. . .

. . . The present German submarine warfare against commerce is a warfare against mankind.

It is a war against all nations. . . .

The challenge is to all mankind. Each nation must decide for itself how it will meet it. The choice we make for ourselves must be made with a moderation of counsel and a temperateness for judgement befitting our character and our motives as a nation. We must put excited feeling away. Our motive will not be revenge or the victorious assertion of the physical might of the nation, but only the vindication of right, of human right, of which we are only a single champion.

When I addressed the Congress on the twenty-sixth of February last I thought that it would suffice to assert our neutral rights with arms, our right to use the seas against unlawful interference, our right to keep our people safe against unlawful violence.

But armed neutrality, it now appears, is impracticable. . . .

. . . it is likely only to produce what it was meant to prevent; it is practically certain to draw us into the war without either the rights or the effectiveness of belligerents.

There is one choice we cannot make, we are incapable of making: we will not choose the path of submission and suffer the most sacred rights of our Nation and our people to be ignored or violated. The wrongs against which we now array ourselves are no common wrongs; they cut to the very roots of human life.

With a profound sense of the solemn and even tragical character of the step I am taking and of the grave responsibilities which it involves, but in unhesitating obedience to what I deem my constitutional duty, I advise that the Congress declare the recent course of the Imperial German Government to be in fact nothing less than war against the government and people of the United States; that it formally accept the status of belligerent which has thus been thrust upon it; and that it take immediate steps not only to put the country in a more thorough state of defence but also to exert all its power and employ all its resources to bring the Government of the German Empire to terms and end the war.

While we do these things, these deeply momentous things, let us be very clear, and make very clear to all the world what our motives and our objectives are. . . .

. . .

Our object now, as then, is to vindicate the principles of peace and justice in the life of the world as against selfish and autocratic power and to set up amongst the really free and self-governed peoples of the world such a concert of purpose and of action as will henceforth insure the observance of those principles.

Neutrality is no longer feasible or desirable where the peace of the world is involved and the freedom of its people, and the menace to that peace and freedom lies in the existence of autocratic governments backed by organized force which is controlled wholly by their will, not by the will of their people.

We have no quarrel with the German people. We have no feeling towards them but one of sympathy and friendship. It was not upon their impulse that their government acted in entering this war. It was not with their previous knowledge or approval.

It was a war determined upon as wars used to be determined upon in the old, unhappy days when peoples were nowhere consulted by their rules and wars were provoked and waged in the interest of dynasties or of little groups of ambitious men who were accustomed to use their fellow men as pawns and tools.

We are now about to accept gauge of battle with this natural foe to liberty and shall, if necessary, spend the whole force of the nation to check and nullify its pretensions and its power. We are glad, now that we see the facts with no veil of false pretence about them, to fight thus for the ultimate peace of the world and for the liberation of its peoples, the German peoples included: for the rights of nations great and small and the privilege of men everywhere to choose their way of life and of obedience.

The world must be made safe for democracy. Its peace must be planted upon the tested foundations of political liberty. We have no selfish ends to serve. We desire no conquest, no dominion. We seek no indemnities for ourselves, no material compensation for the sacrifices we shall freely make. We are but one of the champions of the rights of mankind. We shall be satisfied when those rights have been made as secure as the faith and the freedom of nations can make them.

...

To such a task we can dedicate our lives and our fortunes, everything that we are and everything that we have, with the pride of those who know that the day has come when America is privileged to spend her blood and her might for the principles that gave her birth and happiness and the peace which she has treasured. God helping her, she can do no other.

Source: http://www.firstworldwar.com/source/usawardeclaration.htm.

Opposition to Wilson's War Message

Speech by Sen. George W. Norris, April 4, 1917

The resolution now before the Senate is a declaration of war. Before taking this momentous step, and while standing on the brink of this terrible vortex, we ought to pause and calmly and judiciously consider the terrible consequences of the step we are about to take. We ought to consider likewise the route we have recently traveled and ascertain whether we have reached our present position in a way that is compatible with the neutral position which we claimed to occupy at the beginning and through the various stages of this unholy and unrighteous war.

No close student of recent history will deny that both Great Britain and Germany have, on numerous occasions since the beginning of the war, flagrantly violated in the most serious manner the rights of neutral vessels and neutral nations under existing international law, as recognized up to the beginning of this war by the civilized world.

. . .

It is unnecessary to cite authority to show that both [German and British] orders declaring military zones [in the seas] were illegal and contrary to international law. It is sufficient to say that our government has officially declared both of them to be illegal and has officially protested against both of them. The only difference is that in the case of Germany we have persisted in our protest, while in the case of England we have submitted.

What was our duty as a government and what were our rights when we were confronted with these extraordinary orders declaring these military zones? First, we could have defied both of them and could have gone to war against both of these nations for this violation of international law and interference with our neutral rights. Second, we had the technical right to defy one and to acquiesce in the other. Third, we could, while denouncing them both as illegal, have acquiesced in them both and thus remained neutral with both sides, although not agreeing with either as to the righteousness of their respective orders. We could have said to American shipowners that, while these orders are both contrary to international law and are both unjust, we do not believe that the provocation is sufficient to cause us to go to war for the defense of our rights as a neutral nation, and, therefore, American ships and American citizens will go into these zones at their own peril and risk.

Fourth, we might have declared an embargo against the shipping from American ports of any merchandise to either one of these governments that persisted in maintaining its military zone. . . . In my judgment, if we had pursued this course, the zones would have been of short duration. . . .

There are a great many American citizens who feel that we owe it as a duty to humanity to take part in this war. Many instances of cruelty and inhumanity can be found on both sides. . . . To my mind, what we ought to have maintained from the beginning was the strictest neutrality. If we had done this, I do not believe we would have been on the verge of war at the present time. . . .

I have no quarrel to find with the man who does not desire our country to remain neutral. While many such people are moved by selfish motives and hopes of gain, I have no doubt but that in a great many instances, through what I believe to be a misunderstanding of the real condition, there are many honest, patriotic citizens who think we ought to engage in this war. . . . I think such people err in judgment and to a great extent have been misled as to the real history and the true facts by the almost unanimous demand of the great combination of wealth that has a direct financial interest in our participation in the war.

We have loaned many hundreds of millions of dollars to the Allies in this controversy. While such action was legal and countenanced by international law, there is no doubt in my mind but the enormous amount of money loaned to the Allies in this country has been instrumental in bringing about a public sentiment in favor of [war]. Through this instrumentality and also through the instrumentality of others who . . . would expect to make millions more if our country can be drawn into the catastrophe, a large number of the great newspapers and news agencies of the country have been controlled and enlisted in the greatest propaganda that the world has ever known to manufacture sentiment in favor of war.

It is now demanded that the American citizens shall be used as insurance policies to guarantee the safe delivery of munitions of war to belligerent nations. The enormous profits of munition manufacturers, stockbrokers, and bond dealers must be still further increased by our entrance into the war. This has brought us to the present moment, when Congress, urged by the President and backed by the artificial sentiment, is about to declare war and engulf our country in the greatest holocaust that the world has ever known.

. . .

We are taking a step today that is fraught with untold danger. We are going into war upon the command of gold. We are going to run the risk of sacrificing millions of our countrymen's lives in order that other countrymen may coin their lifeblood into money. And even if we do not cross the Atlantic and go into the trenches, we are going to pile up a debt that the tolling masses that shall come many generations after us will have to pay. Unborn millions will bend their backs in toil in order to pay for the terrible step we are now about to take.

We are about to do the bidding of wealth's terrible mandate. By our act we will make millions of our countrymen suffer, and the consequences of it may well be that millions of our brethren must shed their lifeblood, millions of broken-hearted women must weep, millions of children must suffer with cold, and millions of babes must die from hunger, and all because we want to preserve the commercial right of American citizens to deliver munitions of war to belligerent nations.

Speech by Sen. Robert M. La Follette, April 4, 1917

Mr. President, many of my colleagues on both sides of this floor have from day to day offered for publication in the *Record* messages and letters received from their constituents. I have received some 15,000 letters and telegrams. They have come from forty-four states in the Union. They have been assorted according to whether they speak in criticism or commendation of my course in opposing war. Assorting the 15,000 letters and telegrams by states in that way, 9 out of 10 are an unqualified endorsement of my course in opposing war with Germany on the issue presented. . . .

Do not these messages indicate on the part of the people a deep-seated conviction that the United States should not enter the European war? . . .

. . .

Sir, if we are to enter upon this war in the manner the President demands, let us throw pretense to the winds, let us be honest, let us admit that this is a ruthless war against not only Germany's Army and her Navy but against her civilian population as well, and frankly state that the purpose of Germany's hereditary European enemies has become our purpose.

. . .

Countless millions are suffering from want and privation; countless other millions are dead and rotting on foreign battlefields; countless other millions are crippled and maimed, blinded, and dismembered; upon all and upon their children's children for generations to come has been laid a burden of debt which must be worked out in poverty and suffering, but the "whole force" of no one of the warring nations has yet been expended; but our "whole force" shall be expended, so says the President. We are pledged by the President, so far as he can pledge us, to make this fair, free, and happy land of ours the same shambles and bottomless pit of horror that we see in Europe today.

Just a word of comment more upon one of the points in the President's address. He says that this is a war "for the things which we have always carried nearest to our hearts—for democracy, for the right of those who submit to authority to have a voice in their own government." In many places throughout the address is this exalted sentiment given expression.

It is a sentiment peculiarly calculated to appeal to American hearts and, when accompanied by acts consistent with it, is certain to receive our support; but in this same connection, and strangely enough, the President says that we have become convinced that the German government as it now exists— "Prussian autocracy" he calls it—can never again maintain friendly relations with us. . . .

But the President proposes alliance with Great Britain, which, however liberty-loving its people, is a hereditary monarchy, . . . with a limited and restricted suffrage for one class and a multiplied suffrage power for another, and with grinding industrial conditions for all the wageworkers. The President has not suggested that we make our support of Great Britain conditional to her granting home rule to Ireland, or Egypt, or India. We rejoice in the establishment of a democracy in Russia, but it will hardly be contended that if Russia was still an autocratic government, we would not be asked to enter this alliance with her just the same.

Who has registered the knowledge or approval of the American people of the course this Congress is called upon to take in declaring war upon Germany? Submit the question to the people, you who support it. You who support it dare not do it, for you know that by a vote of more than ten to one the American people as a body would register their declaration against it.

In the sense that this war is being forced upon our people without their knowing why and without their approval, and that wars are usually forced upon all peoples in the same way, there is some truth in the statement; but I venture to say that the response which the German people have made to the demands of this war shows that it has a degree of popular support which the war upon which we are entering has not and never will have among our people. The espionage bills, the conscription bills, and other forcible military measures which we understand are being ground out of the war machine in this country is the complete proof that those responsible for this war fear that it has no popular support and that armies sufficient to satisfy the demand of the Entente Allies cannot be recruited by voluntary enlistments. . . .

. . .

It is not my purpose to go into detail into the violations of our neutrality by any of the belligerents. While Germany has again and again yielded to our protests, I do not recall a single instance in which a protest we have made to Great Britain has won for us the slightest consideration, except for a short time in the case of cotton. I will not stop to dwell upon the multitude of minor violations of our neutral rights, such as seizing our mails, violations of the neutral flag, seizing and appropriating our goods without the least warrant or authority in law, and impressing, seizing, and taking possession of our vessels and putting them into her own service.

. . .

The only reason why we have not suffered the sacrifice of just as many ships and just as many lives from the violation of our rights by the war zone and the submarine mines of Great Britain as we have through the unlawful acts of Germany in making her war zone in violation of our neutral rights is simply because we have submitted to Great Britain's dictation. If our ships had been sent into her forbidden highsea war zone as they have into the proscribed area Germany marked out on the high seas as a war zone, we would have had the same loss of life and property in the one case as in the other; but because we avoided doing that, in the case of England, and acquiesced in her violation of law, we have not only a legal but a moral responsibility for the position in which Germany has been placed by our collusion and cooperation with Great Britain. By suspending the rule with respect to neutral rights in Great Britain's case, we have been actively aiding her in starving the civil population of Germany. We have helped to drive Germany into a corner, her back to the wall to fight with what weapons she can lay her hands on to prevent the starving of her women and children, her old men and babes.

. . .

The failure to treat the belligerent nations of Europe alike, the failure to reject the unlawful "war zones" of both Germany and Great Britain is wholly accountable for our present dilemma. We should not seek to hide our blunder behind the smoke of battle, to inflame the mind of our people by half truths into the frenzy of war in order that they may never appreciate the real cause of it until it is too late. I do not believe that our national honor is served by such a course. The right way is the honorable way.

One alternative is to admit our initial blunder to enforce our rights against Great Britain as we have enforced our rights against Germany; demand that both those nations shall respect our neutral rights upon the high seas to the letter; and give notice that we will enforce those rights from that time forth against both belligerents and then live up to that notice.

The other alternative is to withdraw our commerce from both. The mere sug-
gestion that food supplies would be withheld from both sides impartially
would compel belligerents to observe the principle of freedom of the seas for
neutral commerce.

Source: http://www.mtholyoke.edu/acad/intrel/doc19.htm.

Alternate Realities

Instructions: Review the three speeches and answer the following questions. Be prepared to evaluate each speaker's assertions.

1. What reasons did Wilson give for going to war?

2. Why did his opponents think the United States was going to war?

3. What alternative policies did Wilson's opponents suggest?

4. What did his opponents see as reasons for not becoming involved?

Copyright ©2009 by International Debate Education Association
The Publisher grants permission for the reproduction of this worksheet except for commercial purposes.
Activity sheets may be downloaded from www.idebate.org/handouts.htm

14. Women's Suffrage

INSTRUCTIONAL OBJECTIVES

Students will be able to:

- Explain how women achieved the vote
- Understand the contemporary arguments presented for and against suffrage
- Understand the cultural dimensions behind the arguments

DESCRIPTION

Working in small groups, students will develop a campaign to promote women's suffrage at the beginning of the 20th century.

TIME

Two class periods

MATERIALS

Women's Suffrage Chronology (copy for each student)
Debating Suffrage (copy for each student)
On to Victory! (copy for each student)

CLASS LAYOUT AND GROUPING OF STUDENTS

Students will work in small groups to prepare their campaigns. The class will hear and debate the campaign plans in their usual seating assignments.

PROCEDURE

Day 1:

1. Explain that the campaign for women's suffrage stretched from the Seneca Falls Convention of 1848 into the 20th century. Distribute Women's Suffrage Chronology and present a short overview of 19th century developments, emphasizing the following:
   - Women's suffrage was a radical idea even to those at the Seneca Falls Convention
   - Supporters of women's rights and abolitionists worked together to further both goals until the Civil War prompted the two groups to focus on emancipation
   - The postwar debate over who should get priority (women or male African Americans) in the campaign for voting rights ends the alliance between former abolitionists and women's rights activists, and splits the women's rights movement. The National

Woman Suffrage Association, which opposed the emphasis on black male suffrage at the expense of women, supported a constitutional amendment granting women the vote; the American Woman Suffrage Association, which reluctantly accepted prioritizing black male voting, supported campaigns to win the vote at the state level
- The two groups reunite at the end of the 19th century, and the reenergized movement pushes for suffrage.

2. Explain that the class will go back to the turn of the 20th century. They will divide into groups to plan a campaign the women's movement will use to win the vote. To do this they must analyze the strategies of earlier campaigns to see what worked and what didn't. They must also analyze arguments for and against suffrage, to counter opponents and deliver their most powerful message. Warn the class that they must stay in the early 20th century—no text messaging or YouTube ads, no pointing to women as successful governors! Each group will develop a detailed campaign that it will present and justify to the other groups.

3. Organize the class into groups of five to six and distribute Debating Suffrage. Tell them they are to begin by using Women's suffrage Chronology and Debating Suffrage to analyze what had been done to further the cause, and to understand the arguments for and against suffrage. They are then to develop a campaign to achieve suffrage. Tell the class that the campaign must be detailed and include strategy and tactics: Are they recommending a state-by-state campaign or a focus on a constitutional amendment? What tactics will they use (lobbying politicians, writing articles, etc.)? Remind them that the tactics must be appropriate for the early 20th century. Tell them that each group will have five minutes to present their campaign

Day 2:
1. Ask a spokesperson from each group to present their recommendations. Note these on the board. After each group presents, ask the class if they have any questions about the campaign. Monitor the presentation closely to ensure that the groups are not basing their campaigns on inaccurate information. For example, given the chronology, groups might suggest an alliance with the Populists, but that movement had died out by the beginning of the 20th century.

2. Once all groups have presented, ask the class to evaluate each campaign.

3. Close by summarizing the campaign suffragists used to win passage of the Nineteenth Amendment.

ASSESSMENT
You can assess the students during the group presentations and discussion.

EXTENSIONS AND MODIFICATIONS

Explain that women's struggle for equality did not end with suffrage. In 1923, Alice Paul, one of the leaders of the suffrage movement, first proposed the Equal Rights Amendment to the U.S. Constitution, which simply stated that "Equality of rights under the law shall not be denied or abridged by the United States or by any State on account of sex." The proposal won little public support until the National Organization for Women took up the crusade for passage in 1967. Although Congress passed the amendment, it did not win ratification due to conservative opposition. Ask the class to debate whether or not this amendment is still needed.

Women's Suffrage Chronology

1848 The First Women's Rights Convention takes place in Seneca Falls, New York. Among the demands in the convention's "Declaration of Sentiments" is the radical request for women's suffrage.

1850 The first National Women's Rights Convention meets in Worcester, Massachusetts. A strong alliance is formed with the abolitionist movement.

1861–1865 During the Civil War, women suspend their campaign for suffrage to put their energies toward the war effort. At the end of the war, many women's rights activists are optimistic that the federal government will reward them with the vote for the contributions and sacrifices women made to the Union cause.

1866 Elizabeth Cady Stanton and Susan B. Anthony form the American Equal Rights Association (AERA) to further the goal of suffrage for all, regardless of gender or race.

1868 AERA begins to divide over support for the Fourteenth Amendment, which defines "citizens" and "voters" exclusively as male.

1869 AERA formally splits over the Fifteenth Amendment, which enfranchises black American males while avoiding the question of women's suffrage. Elizabeth Cady Stanton and Susan B. Anthony bitterly oppose the amendment, and establish the National Woman Suffrage Association (NWSA) to achieve the vote through a constitutional amendment, and to push for other women's rights issues. More conservative activists, led by Lucy Stone and Julia Ward Howe, reluctantly support the Fifteenth Amendment. They form the American Woman Suffrage Association (AWSA), which focuses on suffrage through amending individual state constitutions.

1869 Hoping that the resulting publicity will bring women to Wyoming (where the ratio of men to women was six to one), the Wyoming territorial legislature enacts a law granting women's suffrage.

1870 Convinced that granting women's suffrage will reduce Congressional hostility to Mormon polygamy, male politicians in the Utah territory give women the vote.

1872 Suffragists file court challenges to test the constitutionality of existing election laws. Arguing that the Fourteenth and Fifteenth Amendments guarantee their right to vote as citizens, women present themselves at the polls to vote in a number of states. Susan B. Anthony attempts to vote, in an effort to bring the issue to the Supreme Court. She is arrested and brought to trial in Rochester, New York. Anthony is fined, but the case does not move to the high court. Virginia Minor, a former president of the Missouri Woman Suffrage Association, also tries to register to vote in 1872, and is denied. She sues the registrar on the grounds that her being denied the opportunity to vote is an infringement on her civil rights under the Fourteenth Amendment.

1874 Annie Wittenmyer founds the Woman's Christian Temperance Union (WCTU). Convinced that only the vote will give women the power to make social change, the WCTU becomes an important proponent in the fight for women's suffrage. As a result, one of the strongest opponents to women's enfranchisement was the liquor lobby.

1875 In the case *Minor v. Happersett* (1875), the Supreme Court rules against Minor, determining that the Fourteenth Amendment does not grant women the vote. After this decision, the suffrage movement directs its campaign to winning the franchise at the state level. The movement makes the West the primary focus of its operations.

1878 A Woman Suffrage Amendment (the Anthony Amendment) is proposed in the U.S. Congress. When the Nineteenth Amendment passes 41 years later, it is worded exactly the same as this amendment.

1882 The House and Senate appoint committees on women's suffrage; both report favorably.

1887 In the Senate, a vote on women's suffrage is defeated by a two-to-one margin.

1890 NWSA and AWSA merge, forming the National American Woman Suffrage Association. The movement focuses on securing suffrage at the state level.

The South Dakota campaign for women's suffrage loses.

ca. 1890 The Progressive Era begins. Women from all classes and backgrounds begin entering public life and consequently the issue of women's suffrage enters mainstream politics.

1893 Benefiting from Populist support for women's suffrage, and arguing that a vote for women would be a vote against the corporations and railroads, women win suffrage in Colorado.

1894 Despite 600,000 signatures presented to the New York State Constitutional Convention, suffragists fail in their effort to bring a women's suffrage amendment to the voters.

1896 Idaho, where a large number of women have participated in the Populist movement, adopts women's suffrage.

Copyright ©2009 by International Debate Education Association
The Publisher grants permission for the reproduction of this worksheet except for commercial purposes. Activity sheets may be downloaded from www.idebate.org/handouts.htm

Debating Suffrage

PRO-SUFFRAGE ARGUMENTS

- In a republic, women, as human beings, deserve the same individual rights owed to men.

- Women can and should participate beyond the private sphere of the home, providing a moral vote on issues that they traditionally dominate.

- Women are morally superior to men, and as such a vote for women is a vote for a better America. Women will support Progressive reforms such as prohibition, child labor, pure food laws, and industrial legislation.

- The vote would enable women to have a say in the issues that directly affect them and the family. Since women dominate the private sphere and are directly affected by government regulations that pertain to family, children, and home, they should be able to vote for the government officials who make those regulations.

- Allowing women to vote will clean up politics. Women are naturally non-partisan and morally superior. Therefore they will counter political corruption.

- (Argument used in the South) The vote for women (at least white women) will offset the vote of black men and guarantee the continuation of white supremacy.

ANTI-SUFFRAGE ARGUMENTS

- By nature men and women are different, and they exist in separate but equal spheres. Women dominate the domestic sphere. Within the home women can effect change without voting by indirectly influencing the male members of their household. Therefore, women do not need the vote. They already have an indirect say in politics.

- Because women are not involved in the corrupt political world, they have no political loyalties. Being nonpartisan, their decision-making is clearer than that of their male counterparts. Thus, women's influence on the male members of their families is the highest level of morality thinking.

- Disrupting the separate spheres would be catastrophic to the family. By removing women from the private sphere of the home and placing them in the public world of dirty politics, you jeopardize American society. If women were to enter politics, they would leave undone the work for which they are called—ministering to life in the home. They cannot do both.

- Women do not want the vote. In 1895 the women of Massachusetts were asked whether they wanted the vote. Of the 575,000 women who voted, only 22,204 said "yes." Women see that suffrage is not merely a political question, but one that would initiate a revolution in American society.

- Women's suffrage will double the cost of the electoral process.

Copyright ©2009 by International Debate Education Association
The Publisher grants permission for the reproduction of this worksheet except for commercial purposes.
Activity sheets may be downloaded from www.idebate.org/handouts.htm

On to Victory!

Instructions: You are meeting at the turn of the 20th century to advise the women's movement on how best to campaign to win the vote. Remember as you write your campaign that you must remain in the early 20th century—no Internet campaigns, no referring to 21st century perceptions of women.

Use Women's Suffrage Chronology and Debating Suffrage to develop an overview of the strategies and tactics suffragists used in the past, and to understand the arguments for and against suffrage. Then develop your campaign recommendations. The campaign must include strategy and detailed tactics. You will have five minutes to present your campaign to the class. Be prepared to defend your recommendations.

Best Strategy (state-by-state; federal amendment; both):

Recommended Tactics (lobbying Congress, letter writing, alliances with other organizations, etc. Remember that you must address arguments against suffrage to further your campaign.)

Copyright ©2009 by International Debate Education Association
The Publisher grants permission for the reproduction of this worksheet except for commercial purposes. Activity sheets may be downloaded from www.idebate.org/handouts.htm

15. The New Deal

INSTRUCTIONAL OBJECTIVES
Students will be able to:
- Explain how the New Deal addressed the Great Depression, transformed American federalism, and initiated an era of Big Government
- Articulate the factors underlying New Deal reform
- Evaluate the success and failures of the relief, recovery, and reform measures
- Assess the long-term impact of the New Deal on American government and society

DESCRIPTION
Students will work in small groups to research some of the most important New Deal agencies. They will determine why the agency was founded, evaluate its achievements, and assess its long-term impact. They will then present their findings to the class, who will analyze the information to determine the common elements underlying New Deal reform.

TIME
One period for research; one period for discussion

MATERIALS
Alphabet Agencies (copy for each student)

PREPARATION
Reserve the computer lab.

CLASS LAYOUT AND GROUPING OF STUDENTS
Students will work in small groups around the computers and assume their usual seating arrangements for presentations and discussion.

PROCEDURE
Part 1: Research
1. Review the situation in the United States when Franklin D. Roosevelt (FDR) assumed the presidency. Emphasize the following:

    More than 25 percent of the population was unemployed, industrial production had fallen by more than 50 percent in less than four years, two million people who had recently enjoyed a comfortable life were now homeless, and farmers were struggling as prices for their crops had plummeted by 60 percent.

2. Explain that Roosevelt, to combat the Depression, implemented the most significant program of liberal reform in American history. The program dramatically changed government and the way Americans viewed the federal government. It shifted the center of politics from states and localities to the federal government, which became responsible for steering the economy, promoting social welfare, regulating labor relations, and curbing the abuses of business. Henceforth, Americans would expect the federal government to assure prosperity and help those unable to help themselves.

3. Explain that the Roosevelt administration ushered in the era of Big Government in American history, by establishing a large number of agencies and commissions to carry out FDR's programs. These were called Alphabet Agencies because they were usually known by their acronyms (AAA, WPA, etc.). Tell the students that they will investigate these agencies to determine whether or not they were effective in achieving Roosevelt's goals, and whether they had a long-term impact on American society and government.

4. Divide the class into small groups, distribute Alphabet Agencies, and assign an agency to each group. You may use some or all of the agencies listed below, or others of your choice.
    Agricultural Adjustment Administration
    Civilian Conservation Corps
    Civil Works Administration
    Federal Emergency Relief Administration
    National Recovery Administration
    Public Works Administration
    Securities and Exchange Commission
    Social Security Administration
    Tennessee Valley Authority

    Tell the students to research the questions on the handout, then prepare a short presentation on the agency to share with the class.

Part 2: Presentation and Analysis
1. Ask each group to present its overview of the agency. As the students do so, fill in the following chart on the board.

Name of agency	Date established	Reason for founding/ goals	Achieve- ments	Did the agency ful- fill its goals?	Long- term impact

2. Ask the class whether their research has revealed any common elements or attitudes behind New Deal programs. Point out that historians have suggested that the New Deal was grounded in:
   - Pragmatism and bold experimentation
   - A commitment to use the power of the federal government as a counterweight to big business
   - A commitment to provide government assistance to those who could not fend for themselves in the private economy
   - A belief that government could actively engage in economic planning without creating a regimented economy or stifling initiative

ASSESSMENT

You may assess the presentations or ask the groups to prepare a paper based on their research for evaluation.

EXTENSIONS AND MODIFICATIONS

- If you wish to analyze the First and Second New Deals, call on the groups in the order in which the agencies were founded, then ask the students to contrast policy-making in the two periods.
- Debate whether the Big Government Roosevelt established has been beneficial for the nation.
- Point out that the New Deal engendered vigorous opposition. Former president Herbert Hoover warned that it "violated principles which reach to the very foundation of our nation." Ask the class to debate this assertion.

Alphabet Agencies

Instructions: Answer the following questions about your New Deal agency and use that information to develop a short presentation on the agency for the class.

Name of agency:_____

Date established:_____

Why did Roosevelt establish the agency?

What problems was the agency to address? What were the agency's goals?

What were the agency's achievements?

Did the agency achieve Roosevelt's goals?

What was the long-term impact of the agency beyond the New Deal era?

Copyright ©2009 by International Debate Education Association
The Publisher grants permission for the reproduction of this worksheet except for commercial purposes.
Activity sheets may be downloaded from www.idebate.org/handouts.htm

16. Truman and the Atom Bomb

INSTRUCTIONAL OBJECTIVES
Students will be able to:
- Evaluate Truman's decision to use the atom bomb
- Understand the historical circumstances in which Truman made his decision

DESCRIPTION
Students will evaluate the arguments for and against using the atomic bomb, and they will debate the wisdom of Truman's decision.

TIME
60 minutes

MATERIALS
Arguments (copy for each student)

CLASS LAYOUT AND GROUPING OF STUDENTS
Students will remain in their usual seating arrangement for the discussion.

PROCEDURE
1. Explain that Harry Truman's decision to use the atom bomb against Japan in the closing days of the war remains one of the most controversial presidential acts in American history. Tell the students that they will analyze the arguments presented for and against the bomb's use and debate whether Truman made the best choice.

2. Set the stage for the debate, explaining the historical context in which Truman had to make his decision. The war in Europe had ended and the defeat of Japan seemed inevitable. Its navy and air force had been destroyed, but the Japanese appeared ready to fight to the last man to defend their home islands. With victory achieved in Europe, Stalin was contemplating entering the war in the Pacific. Truman had to decide whether to use the bomb and under what circumstances.

3. Distribute Arguments and ask the class to review and evaluate the strengths and weaknesses of each argument. Ask students to add any other arguments they think important.

They should be prepared to defend their position in a debate with the entire class. Tell the class they have 20 minutes to make their evaluation.

4. Once the class has analyzed the arguments, ask the students to stand and divide into those who support and those who oppose Truman's decision. Ask one member of the group who supports Truman to come to the front of the class to present what he or she thinks is an important argument for using the bomb, then defend that choice. Ask a member of the group opposing Truman's choice to come forward, counter that argument and present an argument in opposition to Truman. Continue this process until the class has reviewed all arguments.

5. Ask the class if, in light of the discussion, anyone wishes to change sides. Have the class again divide pro and con.

6. Ask the students to return to their seats and summarize the factors behind Truman's decision. Tell the class that Truman never regretted using the bomb.

ASSESSMENT

You can assess the students as they present and defend their arguments pro and con.

EXTENSIONS AND MODIFICATIONS

Explain to the class that when J. Robert Oppenheimer, the scientific director of the Manhattan Project, saw the first mushroom cloud, he recalled the *Bagavad Gita*: "I am become death, the shatterer of worlds." Ask the class to evaluate the long-term consequences of unleashing atomic power in light of the quote.

Arguments

Pro	Con
• Japan attacked Pearl Harbor.	• We do not need the bomb. The Soviets are about to declare war against Japan. This might convince the Japanese to surrender unconditionally.
• Japan has tortured American prisoners of war.	
• Japan has refused unconditional surrender.	• A blockade of Japan along with continued conventional bombing might eventually lead to surrender without endangering American troops.
• Using the bomb will shorten the war.	
• Using the bomb would have a profound psychological effect on the Japanese, empowering those Japanese advocating for peace and weakening military resistance.	• The firebombing of Tokyo killed some 100,000 people in a single night, and yet Japan did not surrender.
	• Japan may have been prepared to surrender conditionally—if it could keep the emperor.
• Using the bomb would diminish the need for Soviet help in concluding the war in the Pacific—and intimidate Stalin.	• Releasing the bomb would turn the world against us.
• If the United States were to invade the Japanese home islands, hundreds of thousands of American and Japanese lives would be lost. The campaign to take the small island of Okinawa had resulted in the deaths of more than 12,000 Americans and over 200,000 Japanese and Okinawans.	• We can publically demonstrate the bomb in an isolated site where no one will be hurt.
	• Using the bomb would inevitably lead to a nuclear arms race.
	• Using the bomb, regardless of circumstances, is immoral.
• The U.S. spent $2 billion developing the bomb. If the American people find out that we had the weapon but did not use it to shorten the war and avoid American casualties, they will be furious.	

Pro	Con

Using the bomb without demonstration

- The Japanese would be empowered if the United States demonstrated the bomb and it was a dud

- A demonstration of the bomb at an isolated site would give the Japanese warning. They could intercept the plane carrying the bomb or move American prisoners of war to possible attack sites.

- There were only two bombs—we cannot risk a demonstration.

- If the Japanese were warned, the shock value of the weapon would be lost.

Copyright ©2009 by International Debate Education Association
The Publisher grants permission for the reproduction of this worksheet except for commercial purposes. Activity sheets may be downloaded from www.idebate.org/handouts.htm

Chapter 5
Contemporary United States

In this chapter students explore key topics in contemporary America. It begins with an overview of the Rights Revolution and an analysis of Lyndon Johnson's decision to escalate the Vietnam War. The final two lessons ask students to take a broad view of American history. First, they debate the relationship between rights and security in wartime. Finally, they utilize what they have learned to compare life at the beginning of the 20th century with that in contemporary America.

17. Rights Revolution

INSTRUCTIONAL OBJECTIVES
Students will be able to:
- Recognize and analyze the dramatic growth of civil rights and liberties in the mid-20th century
- Understand the role the Supreme Court played in extending rights and liberties
- Evaluate other forces behind the growth

DESCRIPTION
Students will work in small groups to develop in-depth presentations tracing the dramatic growth in civil liberties and rights during the Rights Revolution of the mid-20th century.

TIME
Three class periods (you may give the groups more time to prepare their reports if necessary)

MATERIALS
Rights Revolution (appropriate copy for each member of the groups)

PREPARATION
Reserve the computer lab.

CLASS LAYOUT AND GROUPING OF STUDENTS
Students will work in small groups in the computer lab to research their material and develop their presentations. The class will be in its usual seating arrangement for the presentation and discussion.

PROCEDURE
Day 1:
1. Tell the class that in the years 1946–1975, the United States saw an unprecedented expansion in the protection of civil liberties and rights in a wide variety of areas, including:
   - freedom of speech and religion
   - criminal rights

- equal protection from discrimination based on race and gender

2. Explain that this expansion was facilitated by the following factors:
    - Supreme Court decisions that reflected a more activist view of the Court, and a changing judicial philosophy that resulted in the development of the incorporation doctrine requiring states to abide by almost all of the major provisions of the Bill of Rights
    - activist organizations such as the ACLU, and civil and women's rights organizations such as the NAACP and NOW
    - Liberal Congresses and presidents receptive to protecting rights
    - Changes in American society

    Present a brief overview of these factors to the class.

3. Tell the class that they will work in groups to trace the history of this expansion in depth. Each group will research one area of civil rights/liberties and develop a short written presentation and timeline tracing its evolution and expansion. Once the groups have finished developing their written presentations, a representative of each group will give an oral overview and distribute the material. Members of the group will then be available to answer any questions the class may have.

4. Organize the class into five groups and assign each a category. Tell them that they can begin their project by researching the laws and Supreme Court decisions on the activity sheet, but that they must go further and research other factors—important groups, changing political or social conditions—that may have impacted the evolution of the rights they are studying.

5. Tell the groups to begin their research.

Day 2:
Ask the groups to finish their research and develop their overviews and timelines and submit them to you for review and duplication. You may give the groups more time if necessary.

Day 3:
1. Ask a representative of each group to present the group's key findings and distribute the material.

2. Once the groups have completed their presentation, facilitate a discussion of the common factors behind the Rights Revolution.

ASSESSMENT
You can assess the groups' written presentations.

EXTENSIONS AND MODIFICATIONS

- You may expand the activity by including a review of the development of the right to privacy, using the following to initiate the research:

    Eisenstadt v. Baird

    Griswold v. Connecticut

    Roe v. Wade

    Skinner v. Oklahoma

- Ask the class to research any limitations on rights since the Rights Revolution.

Rights Revolution: Free Speech

Instructions: You are to work with the other members of your group to develop a short written presentation (no more than three pages) and a timeline tracing the evolution and expansion of freedom of speech, which you will share with the entire class. One member of your group will introduce the material with a three- to five-minute overview. The other members of the group will answer any questions the class has about the material.

The Supreme Court played a major role in expanding free speech. Begin your research by investigating the decisions below. Then, broaden your research to include other factors important in extending this right.

You presentation should address:
- Court decisions
- Groups important in advocating for the expansion of free speech
- Political conditions and, if appropriate, laws extending free speech
- Social conditions important in expanding this right

IMPORTANT SUPREME COURT CASES

Brandenburg v. Ohio

Dennis v. United States

Miller v. California

New York Times Co. v. Sullivan

Roth v. United States

United States v. O'Brien

Yates v. United States

Copyright ©2009 by International Debate Education Association
The Publisher grants permission for the reproduction of this worksheet except for commercial purposes. Activity sheets may be downloaded from www.idebate.org/handouts.htm

Rights Revolution: Freedom of Religion

Instructions: You are to work with the other members of your group to develop a short written presentation (no more than three pages) and a timeline tracing the evolution and expansion of freedom of religion, which you will share with the entire class. One member of your group will introduce the material with a three- to five-minute overview. The other members of the group will answer any questions the class has about the material.

The Supreme Court played a major role in expanding freedom of religion. Begin your research by investigating the decisions below. Then, broaden your research to include other factors important in extending this right.

You presentation should address:
- Court decisions
- Groups important in advocating for expansion of freedom of religion
- Political conditions and, if appropriate, laws extending freedom of religion
- Social conditions important in expanding this right

IMPORTANT SUPREME COURT CASES

Abington Township School District v. Schempp

Cantwell v. Connecticut

Engel v. Vitale

Everson v. Board of Education

Lemon v. Kurtzman

Sherbert v. Verner

Walz v. Tax Commission of the City of New York

Wisconsin v. Yoder

Copyright ©2009 by International Debate Education Association
The Publisher grants permission for the reproduction of this worksheet except for commercial purposes.
Activity sheets may be downloaded from www.idebate.org/handouts.htm

Rights Revolution: Rights of the Accused

Instructions: You are to work with the other members of your group to develop a short written presentation (no more than three pages) and a timeline tracing the evolution and expansion of freedom of the rights of the accused, which you will share with the entire class. One member of your group will introduce the material with a three- to five-minute overview. The other members of the group will answer any questions the class has about the material.

The Supreme Court played a major role in expanding the rights of the accused. Begin your research by investigating the decisions below. Then, broaden your research to include other factors important in extending this right.

You presentation should address:
- Court decisions
- Groups important in advocating for the expansion of the rights of the accused
- Political conditions and, if appropriate, laws extending the rights of the accused
- Social conditions important in expanding this right

IMPORTANT SUPREME COURT CASES

Benton v. Maryland

Duncan v. Louisiana

Escobedo v. Illinois

Furman v. Georgia

Gideon v. Wainwright

Gregg v. Georgia

Griffin v. California

Malloy v. Hogan

Miranda v. Arizona

Robinson v. California

Copyright ©2009 by International Debate Education Association
The Publisher grants permission for the reproduction of this worksheet except for commercial purposes. Activity sheets may be downloaded from www.idebate.org/handouts.htm

Rights Revolution: Civil Rights and Liberties for Minorities

Instructions: You are to work with the other members of your group to develop a short written presentation (no more than three pages) and a timeline tracing the evolution and expansion of freedom of civil rights and liberties for minorities, which you will share with the entire class. One member of your group will introduce the material with a three- to five-minute overview. The other members of the group will answer any questions the class has about the material.

The Supreme Court played a major role in expanding civil rights and liberties for minorities, as did Congress. Begin your research by investigating the decisions and laws below. Then, broaden your research to include other factors important in extending this right.

You presentation should address:
- Court decisions
- Groups important in advocating for the expansion of minority rights
- Political conditions and, if appropriate, laws extending minority rights
- Social conditions important in expanding this right

IMPORTANT SUPREME COURT CASES AND LAWS

Boynton v. Virginia

Brown v. Board of Education

Civil Rights Act 1964

Harper v. State Board of Elections

Loving v. Virginia

Shelley v. Kraemer

South Carolina v. Katzenbach

Swann v. Charlotte-Mecklenburg Board of Education

Sweatt v. Painter

Voting Rights Act 1965

Copyright ©2009 by International Debate Education Association
The Publisher grants permission for the reproduction of this worksheet except for commercial purposes.
Activity sheets may be downloaded from www.idebate.org/handouts.htm

Rights Revolution: Gender Equality

Instructions: You are to work with the other members of your group to develop a short written presentation (no more than three pages) and a timeline tracing the evolution and expansion of gender equality, which you will share with the entire class. One member of your group will introduce the material with a three- to five-minute overview. The other members of the group will answer any questions the class has about the material.

The Supreme Court and Congress played major roles expanding gender equality. Begin your research by investigating the decisions and laws below. Then, broaden your research to include other factors important in extending gender equality.

You presentation should address:
- Court decisions
- Groups important in advocating for equality for women
- Political conditions and, if appropriate, laws extending equality for women
- Social conditions important in expanding gender equality

IMPORTANT SUPREME COURT CASES AND LAWS
Civil Rights Act 1964

Corning Glass Works v. Brennan

Equal Credit Opportunity Act 1974

Equal Pay Act 1963

Executive Order 11375

Frontiero v. Richardson

Pregnancy Discrimination Act 1978

Reed v. Reed

Schultz v. Wheaton Glass Co.

Title IX of the Education Amendments 1972

Copyright ©2009 by International Debate Education Association
The Publisher grants permission for the reproduction of this worksheet except for commercial purposes.
Activity sheets may be downloaded from www.idebate.org/handouts.htm

18. Vietnam

INSTRUCTIONAL OBJECTIVES

Students will be able to:

- Understand the circumstances leading up to Lyndon Johnson's commitment of ground troops to Vietnam
- Understand the arguments, pro and con, for large-scale U.S. involvement in Vietnam

DESCRIPTION

Students will work in groups to read a background of events that led up to Johnson's decision to Americanize the Vietnam conflict. They will read the views of the Hawks and the Doves and debate in a historical role-play as one side or the other, trying to convince Johnson to engage or to withdraw from Vietnam.

TIME

One or two class periods

MATERIALS

Johnson's Hawks and Doves handout (copy for each student)
Vietnam Involvement Pro and Con (copy for each student)
The Decision to Americanize the War (copy for each student)

CLASS LAYOUT AND GROUPING OF STUDENTS

Students will work in small groups prior to engaging in the point-counterpoint debate involving the entire class.

PROCEDURE

1. Explain that the Vietnam War deeply divided, and still divides, Americans. Tell the students that they will explore the circumstances leading to President Lyndon B. Johnson's decision to commit combat troops to war. They will read a synopsis of the views of those pushing for American intervention, the Hawks, and those opposed, the Doves. Students will then form teams of Hawks or Doves and prepare arguments that they would make to encourage LBJ to take their viewpoint, based on information known at the time.

2. Distribute Johnson's Hawks and Doves. Ask the students to read the background section and discuss. Ensure that the students understand the context in which Johnson made his decision before proceeding.

3. Organize the class into groups of three to four and tell the students that they are now to read the Hawks and Doves sections of the resource sheet.

4. When the groups have finished, distribute Vietnam Involvement Pro and Con. Explain that they are now living and advising in 1965. They are to develop at least five arguments, both pro and con, about large-scale American involvement in Vietnam, and note these arguments on the activity sheet. These arguments must remain in 1965—they cannot refer to events or outcomes that had not yet happened. Explain to the students that they will have 15–20 minutes to work on their arguments. Answer any questions and tell the students to begin working.

5. After 20 minutes, have the students count off by twos. The Ones are Hawks and the Twos are Doves. Explain that the students will now work independently to write a short speech persuading Johnson to accept their viewpoint. The speech should be 1–2 minutes in length, and should incorporate the three best arguments that the student identified. They have 10–12 minutes to write their speeches. When they are finished, they will take part in a Top Secret meeting with President Johnson (you), to try to persuade him to adopt their position on the Vietnam conflict. Circulate as the students work, answering any questions they may have.

6. After they have completed their speeches, call for the students' attention and explain that you are now convening the Top Secret meeting. Explain that you will call on an adviser to present his or her opinion, and will follow up each speech by asking if there are any advisers from the opposing side who want to respond to the point(s) raised. Try to keep to a point-counterpoint format of the speeches by requesting that students respond to the specific points just raised.

7. After the advisers have presented their viewpoints, explain that you have made your decision. Distribute The Decision to Americanize the War to each student as a wrap-up.

ASSESSMENT

Assess the students informally as they present their speeches and respond to the advisers from the opposing side.

EXTENSIONS AND MODIFICATIONS

Debate what the United States learned—if anything—from the experience of Vietnam.

Johnson's Hawks and Doves

(The following is a summary of historical events as published by the U.S. Department of State.)

BACKGROUND

By 1965, fighting between noncommunist South Vietnam, backed primarily by the United States, and North Vietnam, aided by the People's Republic of China and the Soviet Union, had raged for over a decade. The United States had been directly involved since 1954 in only a limited way, sending noncombatant military advisers to help the South Vietnamese Government counter North Vietnam and the communist guerrillas in the south, the National Liberation Front (NLF). Johnson inherited the limited U.S. role in Vietnam when he became President following the assassination of John F. Kennedy in November 1963. But he delayed charting a clear course in Vietnam throughout 1964, in part, because he feared that doing so would damage his candidacy in that year's presidential election. He did obtain congressional approval to prosecute the war. The Tonkin Gulf Resolution, passed in August 1964 after two U.S. vessels operating in the waters off the North Vietnamese coast reported being fired upon, authorized the commander in chief to take "all necessary measures to repel any armed attacks against the forces of the United States and to prevent any further aggression."

Vietnam rose to the fore in the months following Johnson's successful election bid, when it appeared possible that America's ally, South Vietnam, would lose the war. Johnson quickly ruled out abandoning Saigon, an action that he believed would hurt him politically at home and damage U.S. credibility abroad, encouraging communist challenges elsewhere. Instead, after several attempts to shore up the South Vietnamese Government had failed, many administration officials increasingly regarded expanding the U.S. role as the only way to stave off NLF advances and save South Vietnam. In early February 1965, Mc-George Bundy, Special Assistant to the President for National Security Affairs, traveled to South Vietnam to assess the situation and recommend action. During his visit, the NLF attacked a U.S. Army barracks in Pleiku, killing nine Americans. Upon his return to Washington, Bundy informed the president, "The situation in Vietnam is deteriorating, and without new U.S. action defeat appears inevitable." There is still time to turn it around, but not much." The President responded on February 13 by approving Rolling Thunder, a sustained bombing campaign against targets in North Vietnam, designed to improve South Vietnamese morale, complicate the north's infiltration of the south, and force Hanoi to the bargaining table. The expanded air war, in turn, provided the justification for the next significant step on the road to escalation: the introduction of the first U.S. ground forces in Vietnam. On February 26, Johnson dispatched Marine brigades to secure a crucial air base at Danang.

Hawks

To the dismay of Johnson and his foreign policy team, however, these measures failed to turn the war's tide. As a result, in the spring and summer of 1965, they engaged in a heated debate about what course of action to take in Vietnam. Most of Johnson's key advisers argued that only the introduction of substantial numbers of U.S. ground forces would preserve an independent and noncommunist South Vietnam, halt the spread of communism in Southeast Asia, and uphold U.S. credibility. Ambassador to Saigon Gen. Maxwell D. Taylor, Commander of the Military Assistance Command in Vietnam Gen. William C. Westmoreland, Secretary of Defense Robert S. McNamara, and Chairman of the Joint Chiefs of Staff (JCS) Gen. Earle G. Wheeler, among others, met on April 20 in Honolulu, where they recommended the introduction of almost 50,000 additional U.S. troops, bringing the total to about 82,000. McNamara reported these recommendations to President Johnson, explaining that military experts now envisioned a significant offensive role for U.S. troops. The President approved the dispatch of six of the requested nine battalions.

Later, in June, General Westmoreland, whose dispatches from the field first prompted consideration of the issue in Washington, reported that he foresaw a long "war of attrition" developing in Vietnam. And he recommended the deployment of 150,000 additional forces, arguing that such numbers were necessary "to permit the [South] Vietnamese with our help to carry the war to the enemy."

President Johnson and his senior advisers discussed Vietnam during a meeting at the White House on June 23. The attendees were divided, with Undersecretary of State George W. Ball expressing reservations about the administration's ever-deepening commitment. But Secretary of State Dean Rusk sided with the hawks, arguing that, if the United States did not save South Vietnam, the rest of Southeast Asia would fall to communism. Acting on such advice, Johnson ordered additional battalions to Vietnam six days later, pushing the total force level to 125,000.

Even that figure proved insufficient, however, and Westmoreland, Wheeler, and McNamara all advocated a deeper commitment, recommending to President Johnson in July that he expand U.S. forces in Vietnam up to 34 battalions, or 175,000 troops. On July 8, President Johnson received a strong endorsement of his gradual escalation in Vietnam from a panel of distinguished informal presidential advisers, known as the "Wise Men." They advised him that Vietnam represented a crucial Cold War test of the American ability to contain communism. Arguing that the administration, thus far, had been "too restrained," they believed that the stakes were sufficiently high in Vietnam for the President to make "whatever combat force increases were required." Concerned about Congress' willingness to endorse such proposals, the President discussed them during a telephone conversation with Sen. Mike Mansfield, who emerged as a leading critic of the President's policies in Vietnam.

Doves

Not all of Johnson's foreign policy experts supported the deepening U.S. commitment in Vietnam. Adviser Clark Clifford believed that the deployment of U.S. ground forces "should be kept to a minimum." Vietnam, he wrote the President, "could be a quagmire. It could turn into an open end commitment on our part that would take more and more ground troops, without a realistic hope of ultimate victory."

Ball similarly opposed the drive toward a military solution. He instead urged Johnson to limit the commitment of U.S. ground forces. American soldiers, Ball argued on several occasions, would be perceived as foreign invaders by the Vietnamese, both north and south, and would be fighting an unfamiliar guerrilla war on unfamiliar jungle terrain. As a result, he argued, there was little likelihood of success in Vietnam, despite the introduction of more and more U.S. troops. The United States, he proposed, should make the best of a bad situation by cutting its losses and immediately seeking "a way out," meaning a diplomatic settlement. The short-term costs of a negotiated withdrawal would be substantial, he admitted. But the long-term costs of escalating the war would be even greater, he predicted, since the United States would fail even after spending its treasure, its prestige, and its soldiers' lives. Ball posed the question, thusly, "Should we commit U.S. manpower and prestige to a terrain so unfavorable as to give a very large advantage to the enemy—or should we seek a compromise settlement which achieves less than our stated objectives and thus cut our losses while we still have the freedom of maneuver to do so?"

Source: U.S. Secretary of State, "Introductory Essay," http://future.state.gov/educators/lessons/vietnam/43444.htm (accessed August 27, 2008).

Vietnam Argument Pro and Con

Instructions: Read Johnson's Hawks and Doves and develop five arguments pro and five arguments con on escalating U.S. involvement in Vietnam in 1965.

Pro	Con

Copyright ©2009 by International Debate Education Association
The Publisher grants permission for the reproduction of this worksheet except for commercial purposes. Activity sheets may be downloaded from www.idebate.org/handouts.htm

The Decision to Americanize the War

McNamara, who at the President's request visited South Vietnam in early July to determine the potential effect of a large U.S. commitment, provided the clinching argument. McNamara's advice carried particular weight with the President, who had been impressed with his intellect and analytical ability since the early days of the Kennedy administration. Upon his return, the Secretary of Defense again urged the President to increase pressure on Hanoi by augmenting U.S. forces. McNamara foresaw a possible victory in South Vietnam by 1968 if Westmoreland's forces were elevated to the 34-battalion level (about 175,000 U.S. troops) that he had previously recommended. The secretary went even further, though, conceding that an additional 100,000 troops might be needed by early 1966 and advocating calling up 235,000 reservists and National Guardsmen. Ball predicted that such a massive force risked becoming "lost in the rice paddies."

The decision on combat troop deployment came at the July 27 meeting of the National Security Council (NSC). Declaring that the "situation in Vietnam is deteriorating," President Johnson listed the options available to American policymakers: immediate withdrawal, maintaining the present level of U.S. troops, or increasing the U.S. commitment. The President chose to expand the number of U.S. ground troops, approving the immediate deployment of some 75,000 additional forces. But he scaled back the Pentagon's requests, fearing that the all-out commitment they entailed could expand the war by provoking Chinese or Soviet intervention and endanger the Great Society, his cherished domestic reform program. No NSC members, when asked their opinions by Johnson, opposed the decision.

President Johnson's decision Americanized the war by taking the burden of fighting from the South Vietnamese and placing it in the hands of the U.S. military. Recognizing this, Horace Busby, Johnson's political adviser, wrote in July, "This is no longer South Vietnam's war. We are no longer advisers. The stakes are no longer South Vietnam's. The war is ours." President Johnson's decision also launched the United States on its longest and most divisive war that ultimately cost the lives of more than 58,000 Americans. Despite those sacrifices, the United States lost, withdrawing in 1973 from South Vietnam, which only two years later fell to communists backed by North Vietnam. The quagmire in Vietnam, which precipitated antiwar demonstrations in the United States, was so unpopular by 1968 that it destroyed Johnson's political career. The President surprised the nation in March 1968, when he announced that he would not seek the Democratic Party's nomination in that year's presidential election.

Source: U.S. Secretary of State, "Introductory Essay," http://future.state.gov/educators/lessons/vietnam/43444.htm.

19. Rights in Wartime

INSTRUCTIONAL OBJECTIVES

Students will be able to:

- Understand the conflict between rights and security in American history
- Understand the broad context in which basic rights were limited in four episodes in U.S. history
- Evaluate the appropriateness of government action in limiting rights

DESCRIPTION

Students will use four episodes in American history as the basis for a class discussion on the conflict between rights and security in American history.

TIME

60 minutes

MATERIALS

Rights in Wartime (copy for each student)

PREPARATION

Prepare a series of questions that will facilitate and direct the discussion.

CLASS LAYOUT AND GROUPING OF STUDENTS

Students will review the four episodes in their usual seating arrangements, then form a circle for the discussion.

PROCEDURE

1. Explain that during wartime rights guaranteed under the Constitution have often been threatened in the name of national security. The class will review four episodes in which the government limited basic rights and use these episodes as the basis for a discussion of whether restricting rights has been, or ever can be, justified in time of war. Note the discussion topic on the board.

2. Distribute Rights in Wartime and ask the students to review. Answer any questions about the material and summarize the broad context in which each episode took place.

3. Ask the students to think about their position on the issue and to note evidence, either from the examples given or other examples in American history, supporting their stand. Have the students develop one question they would like to ask their colleagues during the discussion.

4. Assemble the desks for the discussion. Emphasize that this is a dialogue, not a debate, and that the goal is to come to a deeper understanding of the topic. Students are to listen closely to their colleagues and to respond to a classmate's statement before presenting their own opinions or questions.

5. Begin the discussion and periodically note the key points that have been discussed. Use your prepared questions to keep the discussion focused. Remember to draw as many students as possible into the discussion.

ASSESSMENT
You can assess the students during the discussion.

EXTENSIONS AND MODIFICATIONS
Ask the class to debate the following quote from Benjamin Franklin: "They who would give up an essential liberty for temporary security, deserve neither liberty or security."

Rights in Wartime

ALIEN AND SEDITION ACTS

The 1790s saw the rise of partisan politics, a development feared by many as threatening the fledgling democracy. Partisan conflict was not yet an accepted element of the political process, and there was a general belief that consensus was necessary for the republic to survive. Political alignments centered around the Federalists (led by Alexander Hamilton), who wanted a strong central government and cooperation with Great Britain, and the Democratic Republicans (led by Thomas Jefferson), who wanted most power to reside with the states rather than the federal government and who were pro-French in their political sympathies.

In response to U.S. ratification of the Jay Treaty of 1796, which provided preferential arrangements with Great Britain, France, then at war with Britain, began attacking American commercial shipping in what became known as the "Quasi War." By 1798, the Federalists, who controlled both the White House and Congress, as well as many Democratic-Republicans anticipated a French invasion. The French had meddled in American politics and had tried to enlist American support for their military causes. Adding to Federalist concern was the presence of thousands of French refugees and Irish immigrants, who might back an invading force. Federalists feared that the French would do so because of their obvious connections to France, while the Irish might be tempted to support France in its war against the long-time enemy of the Irish, Great Britain. In this context, the Federalist Congress passed a series of three laws (Alien Enemies Act, Naturalization Act, and Alien Act) designed to remove potential spies, collaborators, or instigators of domestic unrest, and to limit immigration. A fourth law, the Sedition Act, outlawed both sedition and seditious libel, the latter defined as "false, scandalous, or malicious writing or writings against the Government of the United States, or either House of the Congress . . . or the President . . . with the intent to defame . . . or to bring them . . . into contempt or disrepute." While the alien acts could be construed as national security measures and were lightly applied during the Quasi War, the Naturalization Act, and particularly the Sedition Act, were designed to limit Democratic-Republican support and suppress dissent, and they were used vigorously against Democratic-Republican newspaper editors.

Reaction to the Sedition Act was vigorous and ultimately contributed to the growth of the partisan press. Because the law stipulated that truth was an acceptable defense and that malicious intent had to be proved, the concept of free speech expanded.

ABRAHAM LINCOLN SUSPENDS HABEAS CORPUS

A writ of habeas corpus is a court order requiring the government to bring an accused person before an impartial court to determine whether there is enough evidence to hold the individual against his or her will. The right is central to the U.S. legal system and is guaranteed by the Constitution, which states *The Privilege of the Writ of Habeas Corpus shall not be suspended, unless when in Cases of Rebellion or Invasion the public Safety may require it.*

Within two weeks of the firing on Fort Sumter in April 1861, Lincoln suspended the right of habeas corpus in Maryland, a border state sympathetic to the South that surrounded Washington, D.C. In 1862, fearing the effects of large pockets of antiwar sentiment in the Union, Lincoln suspended habeas corpus and imposed martial law under certain circumstances throughout the nation. The suspension and imposition applied to those who aided the Confederacy, resisted the draft, or were "guilty of any disloyal practice." Those arrested were to be tried and punished by military courts, even though civilian courts were in session. Thousands were arrested, including newspaper editors and speakers critical of the war effort. Lincoln defended his actions, asserting that those opposed to the war endangered public safety. Regular courts, he maintained, were inadequate during an insurrection and would, in any case, release those arrested on a writ of habeas corpus. Thus habeas corpus had to be suspended, and those fomenting trouble incarcerated in order to protect the Union. Chief Justice Roger Taney, sitting as a circuit judge (in that era, Supreme Court justices sat as circuit court justices when the high court was not in session), challenged Lincoln's action in *Ex Parte Merryman* (1861), when he ruled that only Congress had the right to suspend habeas corpus. Lincoln ignored Taney's ruling. Congress later passed the Habeas Corpus Act of 1863, which ratified Lincoln's suspensions and approved future suspensions for the duration of the war.

Lincoln's actions generated widespread criticism, particularly after the arrest and trial of Clement Vallandigham, a prominent Peace Democrat who opposed Lincoln's war policy. Vallandigham was banished to the Confederacy, but supporters asked the Supreme Court to hear his case. In 1864 it refused, saying it had no authority to review the decision of martial law courts. However, the Court did eventually agree to hear a challenge, and in *Ex Parte Milligan* (1866) ruled that there was no justification for martial law, since the ordinary courts had functioned throughout the Civil War. Thus, Lambdin Milligan who had been found guilty of planning rebellion and sentenced to death by a military court, should not have been deprived of his right to habeas corpus. In its decision, the Court noted that "No graver question was ever considered by this court, nor one which more nearly concerns the rights of the whole people."

Japanese-American Internment

In the months following the Japanese attack on Pearl Harbor, pressure mounted from West Coast politicians to "do something" about the Japanese-American population there. Rumors circulated, fueled by race prejudice, that Japanese-Americans were prepared to sabotage the war effort, but an FBI investigation found no grounds for considering them disloyal. Nevertheless, in February 1942 President Franklin D. Roosevelt issued Executive Order 9066, forcing Japanese-Americans to evacuate the West Coast. None had a hearing or trial before being transported to internment camps, and many were forced to sell their property at very low prices. Eventually internment camps held 120,000 persons. Once the internees were in the camps, the government asked them to sign a loyalty oath to the United States. The overwhelming majority did so.

The Supreme Court upheld the legality of the relocation order in *Korematsu v. United States* (1944), ruling that the need to protect against espionage outweighed Korematsu's rights. In dissent Justice Frank Murphy stated that the exclusion of Japanese-Americans "on a plea of military necessity in the absence of martial law ought not to be approved. Such exclusion goes over 'the very brink of constitutional power' and falls into the ugly abyss of racism."

In 1948 Congress partially compensated relocated Japanese-Americans for their loss of property. Forty years later Congress apologized and granted compensation to each surviving prisoner.

WAR ON TERROR

In response to the terrorist attacks of September 11, 2001, Congress and President George W. Bush took several controversial steps in what was called "the war on terror." In October Congress passed, and President Bush signed, the USA PATRIOT Act, which, among other provisions, expanded the power of federal agents to seize records about a person from a third party, such as an Internet service provider or library, and to require the third party to keep the seizure secret. The Act also permitted the indefinite detention of aliens without criminal charges. The law drew instant criticism from both liberals and conservatives, who argued that the Bush administration was using the 9/11 attacks to take away the liberties of the American people.

The following month President Bush issued an order calling for the secretary of defense to detain noncitizens accused of international terrorist acts against the United States or its citizens. Those detained were to be tried by military tribunals in which military officers acted as both judge and jury and determined guilt or innocence by a two-thirds majority vote, rather than the unanimous verdict required in civilian courts. Evidence was admissible if it addressed the case at hand, but the exclusionary rule, which keeps illegally seized evidence out of a civilian criminal trial, did not apply.

In 2006 the Supreme Court ruled in *Hamdan v. Rumsfeld* that the tribunals lacked the power to proceed, because they violated the Geneva Conventions and the U.S. Uniform Code of Military Justice. In response, Congress passed and President Bush signed the Military Commissions Act of 2006, which granted the president almost unlimited authority in establishing and conducting military commissions to try "unlawful enemy combatants" and suspend their right of habeas corpus. Two years later, in *Boumediene v. Bush*, the U.S. Supreme Court ruled that enemy combatants held in U.S. territory are entitled to the writ of habeas corpus and that they may not be detained indefinitely without receiving fair hearings under civilian courts.

Copyright ©2009 by International Debate Education Association
The Publisher grants permission for the reproduction of this worksheet except for commercial purposes.
Activity sheets may be downloaded from www.idebate.org/handouts.htm

20. Past and Present

INSTRUCTIONAL OBJECTIVES

Students will be able to:

- Compare and contrast the United States in 1900 and the contemporary United States
- Evaluate key changes in the United States over the past century
- Synthesize what they have learned to provide a broad picture of the United States "then and now"

DESCRIPTION

Using the example of Ann Nixon Cooper, the centenarian President Barack Obama mentioned in his November 2008 victory speech, the class will review key developments in the United States over the past 100 years.

TIME

60 minutes

MATERIALS

Excerpt, Barack Obama Victory Speech, November 4, 2008

CLASS LAYOUT AND GROUPING OF STUDENTS

Students work in their usual seating arrangements.

PROCEDURE

1. Remind the class that in President Obama's victory speech he mentioned 106-year-old Ann Nixon Cooper to illustrate the changes that America has seen in the past 100 years. Tell the class that Obama mentioned only a few major events and changes in his description. They will now brainstorm to flesh out that description. They are to sketch out what life was like when Ann Nixon Cooper was born, and compare it with life as she experienced it in the contemporary United States.

2. Tell the class that they are not to focus just on rights and liberties, although those should be included, but broadly review how the United States has changed. Ask the class to brainstorm to determine the general categories they should discuss. These might include

rights and liberties, family life, science and technology, health and medicine, government, and major political issues. List these categories on the board.

3. Now ask the class to brainstorm what daily life would have been like for an African-American woman in 1900. Note the answers under the categories. Then ask the class how her life has changed.

ASSESSMENT
You can assess the students as they brainstorm the history.

EXTENSIONS AND MODIFICATIONS
Ask students to debate the opening lines of Barack Obama's victory speech on November 4. "If there is anyone out there who still doubts that America is a place where all things are possible; who still wonders if the dream of our founders is alive in our time; who still questions the power of our democracy, tonight is your answer."

Excerpt, Barack Obama Victory Speech, November 4, 2008

This election had many firsts and many stories that will be told for generations. But one that's on my mind tonight is about a woman who cast her ballot in Atlanta. She's a lot like the millions of others who stood in line to make their voice heard in this election except for one thing—Ann Nixon Cooper is 106 years old.

She was born just a generation past slavery; a time when there were no cars on the road or planes in the sky; when someone like her couldn't vote for two reasons—because she was a woman and because of the color of her skin.

And tonight, I think about all that she's seen throughout her century in America—the heartache and the hope; the struggle and the progress; the times we were told that we can't; and the people who pressed on with that American creed: Yes we can.

At a time when women's voices were silenced and their hopes dismissed, she lived to see them stand up and speak out and reach for the ballot. Yes we can.

When there was despair in the dust bowl and depression across the land, she saw a nation conquer fear itself with a New Deal, new jobs, and a new sense of common purpose. Yes we can.

When the bombs fell on our harbor and tyranny threatened the world, she was there to witness a generation rise to greatness and a democracy was saved. Yes we can.

She was there for the buses in Montgomery, the hoses in Birmingham, a bridge in Selma, and a preacher from Atlanta who told a people that We Shall Overcome. Yes we can.

A man touched down on the moon, a wall came down in Berlin, a world was connected by our own science and imagination. And this year, in this election, she touched her finger to a screen, and cast her vote, because after 106 years in America, through the best of times and the darkest of hours, she knows how America can change. Yes we can.

Source: http://www.huffingtonpost.com/2008/11/04/obama-victory-speech_n_141194.html.

United States Constitution*

We the People of the United States, in Order to form a more perfect Union, establish Justice, insure domestic Tranquility, provide for the common defence, promote the general Welfare, and secure the Blessings of Liberty to ourselves and our Posterity, do ordain and establish this Constitution for the United States of America.

Article. I.

Section. 1.

All legislative Powers herein granted shall be vested in a Congress of the United States, which shall consist of a Senate and House of Representatives.

Section. 2.

The House of Representatives shall be composed of Members chosen every second Year by the People of the several States, and the Electors in each State shall have the Qualifications requisite for Electors of the most numerous Branch of the State Legislature.

No Person shall be a Representative who shall not have attained to the Age of twenty five Years, and been seven Years a Citizen of the United States, and who shall not, when elected, be an Inhabitant of that State in which he shall be chosen.

Representatives and direct Taxes shall be apportioned among the several States which may be included within this Union, according to their respective Numbers, which shall be determined by adding to the whole Number of free Persons, including those bound to Service for a Term of Years, and excluding Indians not taxed, three fifths of all other Persons. The actual Enumeration shall be made within three Years after the first Meeting of the Congress of the United States, and within every subsequent Term of ten Years, in such Manner as they shall by Law direct. The Number of Representatives shall not exceed one for every thirty Thousand, but each State shall have at Least one Representative; and until such enumeration shall be made, the State of New Hampshire shall be entitled to chuse three, Massachusetts eight, Rhode-

---

*Items that are underlined have since been amended or superseded.

Island and Providence Plantations one, Connecticut five, New-York six, New Jersey four, Pennsylvania eight, Delaware one, Maryland six, Virginia ten, North Carolina five, South Carolina five, and Georgia three.

When vacancies happen in the Representation from any State, the Executive Authority thereof shall issue Writs of Election to fill such Vacancies.

The House of Representatives shall chuse their Speaker and other Officers; and shall have the sole Power of Impeachment.

Section. 3.

The Senate of the United States shall be composed of two Senators from each State, <u>chosen by the Legislature</u> thereof for six Years; and each Senator shall have one Vote.

Immediately after they shall be assembled in Consequence of the first Election, they shall be divided as equally as may be into three Classes. The Seats of the Senators of the first Class shall be vacated at the Expiration of the second Year, of the second Class at the Expiration of the fourth Year, and of the third Class at the Expiration of the sixth Year, so that one third may be chosen every second Year; <u>and if Vacancies happen by Resignation, or otherwise, during the Recess of the Legislature of any State, the Executive thereof may make temporary Appointments until the next Meeting of the Legislature, which shall then fill such Vacancies</u>.

No Person shall be a Senator who shall not have attained to the Age of thirty Years, and been nine Years a Citizen of the United States, and who shall not, when elected, be an Inhabitant of that State for which he shall be chosen.

The Vice President of the United States shall be President of the Senate, but shall have no Vote, unless they be equally divided.

The Senate shall chuse their other Officers, and also a President pro tempore, in the Absence of the Vice President, or when he shall exercise the Office of President of the United States.

The Senate shall have the sole Power to try all Impeachments. When sitting for that Purpose, they shall be on Oath or Affirmation. When the President of the United States is tried, the Chief Justice shall preside: And no Person shall be convicted without the Concurrence of two thirds of the Members present.

Judgment in Cases of Impeachment shall not extend further than to removal from Office, and disqualification to hold and enjoy any Office of honor, Trust or Profit under the United States: but the Party convicted shall nevertheless be liable and subject to Indictment, Trial, Judgment and Punishment, according to Law.

Section. 4.

The Times, Places and Manner of holding Elections for Senators and Representatives, shall be prescribed in each State by the Legislature thereof; but the Congress may at any time by Law make or alter such Regulations, except as to the Places of chusing Senators.

The Congress shall assemble at least once in every Year, and such Meeting shall <u>be on the first Monday in December</u>, unless they shall by Law appoint a different Day.

Section. 5.

Each House shall be the Judge of the Elections, Returns and Qualifications of its own Members, and a Majority of each shall constitute a Quorum to do Business; but a smaller Number may adjourn from day to day, and may be authorized to compel the Attendance of absent Members, in such Manner, and under such Penalties as each House may provide.

Each House may determine the Rules of its Proceedings, punish its Members for disorderly Behaviour, and, with the Concurrence of two thirds, expel a Member.

Each House shall keep a Journal of its Proceedings, and from time to time publish the same, excepting such Parts as may in their Judgment require Secrecy; and the Yeas and Nays of the Members of either House on any question shall, at the Desire of one fifth of those Present, be entered on the Journal.

Neither House, during the Session of Congress, shall, without the Consent of the other, adjourn for more than three days, nor to any other Place than that in which the two Houses shall be sitting.

Section. 6.

The Senators and Representatives shall receive a Compensation for their Services, to be ascertained by Law, and paid out of the Treasury of the United States. They shall in all Cases, except Treason, Felony and Breach of the Peace, be privileged from Arrest during their Attendance at the Session of their respective Houses, and in going to and returning from the same; and for any Speech or Debate in either House, they shall not be questioned in any other Place.

No Senator or Representative shall, during the Time for which he was elected, be appointed to any civil Office under the Authority of the United States, which shall have been created, or the Emoluments whereof shall have been encreased during such time; and no Person holding any Office under the

United States, shall be a Member of either House during his Continuance in Office.

Section. 7.

All Bills for raising Revenue shall originate in the House of Representatives; but the Senate may propose or concur with Amendments as on other Bills.

Every Bill which shall have passed the House of Representatives and the Senate, shall, before it become a Law, be presented to the President of the United States: If he approve he shall sign it, but if not he shall return it, with his Objections to that House in which it shall have originated, who shall enter the Objections at large on their Journal, and proceed to reconsider it. If after such Reconsideration two thirds of that House shall agree to pass the Bill, it shall be sent, together with the Objections, to the other House, by which it shall likewise be reconsidered, and if approved by two thirds of that House, it shall become a Law. But in all such Cases the Votes of both Houses shall be determined by yeas and Nays, and the Names of the Persons voting for and against the Bill shall be entered on the Journal of each House respectively. If any Bill shall not be returned by the President within ten Days (Sundays excepted) after it shall have been presented to him, the Same shall be a Law, in like Manner as if he had signed it, unless the Congress by their Adjournment prevent its Return, in which Case it shall not be a Law.

Every Order, Resolution, or Vote to which the Concurrence of the Senate and House of Representatives may be necessary (except on a question of Adjournment) shall be presented to the President of the United States; and before the Same shall take Effect, shall be approved by him, or being disapproved by him, shall be repassed by two thirds of the Senate and House of Representatives, according to the Rules and Limitations prescribed in the Case of a Bill.

Section. 8.

The Congress shall have Power To lay and collect Taxes, Duties, Imposts and Excises, to pay the Debts and provide for the common Defence and general Welfare of the United States; but all Duties, Imposts and Excises shall be uniform throughout the United States;

To borrow Money on the credit of the United States;

To regulate Commerce with foreign Nations, and among the several States, and with the Indian Tribes;

To establish an uniform Rule of Naturalization, and uniform Laws on the subject of Bankruptcies throughout the United States;

To coin Money, regulate the Value thereof, and of foreign Coin, and fix the Standard of Weights and Measures;

To provide for the Punishment of counterfeiting the Securities and current Coin of the United States;

To establish Post Offices and post Roads;

To promote the Progress of Science and useful Arts, by securing for limited Times to Authors and Inventors the exclusive Right to their respective Writings and Discoveries;

To constitute Tribunals inferior to the supreme Court;

To define and punish Piracies and Felonies committed on the high Seas, and Offences against the Law of Nations;

To declare War, grant Letters of Marque and Reprisal, and make Rules concerning Captures on Land and Water;

To raise and support Armies, but no Appropriation of Money to that Use shall be for a longer Term than two Years;

To provide and maintain a Navy;

To make Rules for the Government and Regulation of the land and naval Forces;

To provide for calling forth the Militia to execute the Laws of the Union, suppress Insurrections and repel Invasions;

To provide for organizing, arming, and disciplining, the Militia, and for governing such Part of them as may be employed in the Service of the United States, reserving to the States respectively, the Appointment of the Officers, and the Authority of training the Militia according to the discipline prescribed by Congress;

To exercise exclusive Legislation in all Cases whatsoever, over such District (not exceeding ten Miles square) as may, by Cession of particular States, and the Acceptance of Congress, become the Seat of the Government of the United States, and to exercise like Authority over all Places purchased by the Consent of the Legislature of the State in which the Same shall be, for the Erection of Forts, Magazines, Arsenals, dock-Yards, and other needful Buildings;—And

To make all Laws which shall be necessary and proper for carrying into Execution the foregoing Powers, and all other Powers vested by this Constitution in the Government of the United States, or in any Department or Officer thereof.

Section. 9.

The Migration or Importation of such Persons as any of the States now existing shall think proper to admit, shall not be prohibited by the Congress prior to the Year one thousand eight hundred and eight, but a Tax or duty may be imposed on such Importation, not exceeding ten dollars for each Person.

The Privilege of the Writ of Habeas Corpus shall not be suspended, unless when in Cases of Rebellion or Invasion the public Safety may require it.

No Bill of Attainder or ex post facto Law shall be passed.

No Capitation, or other direct, Tax shall be laid, <u>unless in Proportion to the Census or enumeration herein before directed to be taken</u>.

No Tax or Duty shall be laid on Articles exported from any State.

No Preference shall be given by any Regulation of Commerce or Revenue to the Ports of one State over those of another; nor shall Vessels bound to, or from, one State, be obliged to enter, clear, or pay Duties in another.

No Money shall be drawn from the Treasury, but in Consequence of Appropriations made by Law; and a regular Statement and Account of the Receipts and Expenditures of all public Money shall be published from time to time.

No Title of Nobility shall be granted by the United States: And no Person holding any Office of Profit or Trust under them, shall, without the Consent of the Congress, accept of any present, Emolument, Office, or Title, of any kind whatever, from any King, Prince, or foreign State.

Section. 10.

No State shall enter into any Treaty, Alliance, or Confederation; grant Letters of Marque and Reprisal; coin Money; emit Bills of Credit; make any Thing but gold and silver Coin a Tender in Payment of Debts; pass any Bill of Attainder, ex post facto Law, or Law impairing the Obligation of Contracts, or grant any Title of Nobility.

No State shall, without the Consent of the Congress, lay any Imposts or Duties on Imports or Exports, except what may be absolutely necessary for executing it's inspection Laws: and the net Produce of all Duties and Imposts, laid by any State on Imports or Exports, shall be for the Use of the Treasury of the United States; and all such Laws shall be subject to the Revision and Controul of the Congress.

No State shall, without the Consent of Congress, lay any Duty of Tonnage, keep Troops, or Ships of War in time of Peace, enter into any Agreement or Compact with another State, or with a foreign Power, or engage in War, unless actually invaded, or in such imminent Danger as will not admit of delay.

Article. II.

Section. 1.

The executive Power shall be vested in a President of the United States of America. He shall hold his Office during the Term of four Years, and, together with the Vice President, chosen for the same Term, be elected, as follows:

Each State shall appoint, in such Manner as the Legislature thereof may direct, a Number of Electors, equal to the whole Number of Senators and Representatives to which the State may be entitled in the Congress: but no Senator or Representative, or Person holding an Office of Trust or Profit under the United States, shall be appointed an Elector.

The Electors shall meet in their respective States, and vote by Ballot for two Persons, of whom one at least shall not be an Inhabitant of the same State with themselves. And they shall make a List of all the Persons voted for, and of the Number of Votes for each; which List they shall sign and certify, and transmit sealed to the Seat of the Government of the United States, directed to the President of the Senate. The President of the Senate shall, in the Presence of the Senate and House of Representatives, open all the Certificates, and the Votes shall then be counted. The Person having the greatest Number of Votes shall be the President, if such Number be a Majority of the whole Number of Electors appointed; and if there be more than one who have such Majority, and have an equal Number of Votes, then the House of Representatives shall immediately chuse by Ballot one of them for President; and if no Person have a Majority, then from the five highest on the List the said House shall in like Manner chuse the President. But in chusing the President, the Votes shall be taken by States, the Representation from each State having one Vote; A quorum for this purpose shall consist of a Member or Members from two thirds of the States, and a Majority of all the States shall be necessary to a Choice. In every Case, after the Choice of the President, the Person having the greatest Number of Votes of the Electors shall be the Vice President. But if there should remain two or more who have equal Votes, the Senate shall chuse from them by Ballot the Vice President.

The Congress may determine the Time of chusing the Electors, and the Day on which they shall give their Votes; which Day shall be the same throughout the United States.

No Person except a natural born Citizen, or a Citizen of the United States, at the time of the Adoption of this Constitution, shall be eligible to the Office of President; neither shall any Person be eligible to that Office who shall not have attained to the Age of thirty five Years, and been fourteen Years a Resident within the United States.

In Case of the Removal of the President from Office, or of his Death, Resignation, or Inability to discharge the Powers and Duties of the said Office, the Same shall devolve on the Vice President, and the Congress may by Law provide for the Case of Removal, Death, Resignation or Inability, both of the President and Vice President, declaring what Officer shall then act as President, and such Officer shall act accordingly, until the Disability be removed, or a President shall be elected.

The President shall, at stated Times, receive for his Services, a Compensation, which shall neither be increased nor diminished during the Period for which he shall have been elected, and he shall not receive within that Period any other Emolument from the United States, or any of them.

Before he enter on the Execution of his Office, he shall take the following Oath or Affirmation:—"I do solemnly swear (or affirm) that I will faithfully execute the Office of President of the United States, and will to the best of my Ability, preserve, protect and defend the Constitution of the United States."

Section. 2.

The President shall be Commander in Chief of the Army and Navy of the United States, and of the Militia of the several States, when called into the actual Service of the United States; he may require the Opinion, in writing, of the principal Officer in each of the executive Departments, upon any Subject relating to the Duties of their respective Offices, and he shall have Power to grant Reprieves and Pardons for Offences against the United States, except in Cases of Impeachment.

He shall have Power, by and with the Advice and Consent of the Senate, to make Treaties, provided two thirds of the Senators present concur; and he shall nominate, and by and with the Advice and Consent of the Senate, shall appoint Ambassadors, other public Ministers and Consuls, Judges of the supreme Court, and all other Officers of the United States, whose Appointments are not herein otherwise provided for, and which shall be established by Law: but the Congress may by Law vest the Appointment of such inferior Officers, as they think proper, in the President alone, in the Courts of Law, or in the Heads of Departments.

The President shall have Power to fill up all Vacancies that may happen during the Recess of the Senate, by granting Commissions which shall expire at the End of their next Session.

Section. 3.

He shall from time to time give to the Congress Information of the State of the Union, and recommend to their Consideration such Measures as he shall judge necessary and expedient; he may, on extraordinary Occasions, convene both Houses, or either of them, and in Case of Disagreement between them, with Respect to the Time of Adjournment, he may adjourn them to such Time as he shall think proper; he shall receive Ambassadors and other public Ministers; he shall take Care that the Laws be faithfully executed, and shall Commission all the Officers of the United States.

Section. 4.

The President, Vice President and all civil Officers of the United States, shall be removed from Office on Impeachment for, and Conviction of, Treason, Bribery, or other high Crimes and Misdemeanors.

Article III.

Section. 1.

The judicial Power of the United States shall be vested in one supreme Court, and in such inferior Courts as the Congress may from time to time ordain and establish. The Judges, both of the supreme and inferior Courts, shall hold their Offices during good Behaviour, and shall, at stated Times, receive for their Services a Compensation, which shall not be diminished during their Continuance in Office.

Section. 2.

The judicial Power shall extend to all Cases, in Law and Equity, arising under this Constitution, the Laws of the United States, and Treaties made, or which shall be made, under their Authority;—to all Cases affecting Ambassadors, other public Ministers and Consuls;—to all Cases of admiralty and maritime Jurisdiction;—to Controversies to which the United States shall be a Party;—to Controversies between two or more States;— between a State and Citizens of another State,—between Citizens of different States,—between Citizens of the same State claiming Lands under Grants of different States, and between a State, or the Citizens thereof, and foreign States, Citizens or Subjects.

In all Cases affecting Ambassadors, other public Ministers and Consuls, and those in which a State shall be Party, the supreme Court shall have original Jurisdiction. In all the other Cases before mentioned, the supreme Court shall have appellate Jurisdiction, both as to Law and Fact, with such Exceptions, and under such Regulations as the Congress shall make.

The Trial of all Crimes, except in Cases of Impeachment, shall be by Jury; and such Trial shall be held in the State where the said Crimes shall have been committed; but when not committed within any State, the Trial shall be at such Place or Places as the Congress may by Law have directed.

Section. 3.

Treason against the United States, shall consist only in levying War against them, or in adhering to their Enemies, giving them Aid and Comfort. No Person shall be convicted of Treason unless on the Testimony of two Witnesses to the same overt Act, or on Confession in open Court.

The Congress shall have Power to declare the Punishment of Treason, but no Attainder of Treason shall work Corruption of Blood, or Forfeiture except during the Life of the Person attainted.

Article. IV.

Section. 1.

Full Faith and Credit shall be given in each State to the public Acts, Records, and judicial Proceedings of every other State. And the Congress may by general Laws prescribe the Manner in which such Acts, Records and Proceedings shall be proved, and the Effect thereof.

Section. 2.

The Citizens of each State shall be entitled to all Privileges and Immunities of Citizens in the several States.

A Person charged in any State with Treason, Felony, or other Crime, who shall flee from Justice, and be found in another State, shall on Demand of the executive Authority of the State from which he fled, be delivered up, to be removed to the State having Jurisdiction of the Crime.

No Person held to Service or Labour in one State, under the Laws thereof, escaping into another, shall, in Consequence of any Law or Regulation therein, be discharged from such Service or Labour, but shall be delivered up on Claim of the Party to whom such Service or Labour may be due.

Section. 3.

New States may be admitted by the Congress into this Union; but no new State shall be formed or erected within the Jurisdiction of any other State; nor any State be formed by the Junction of two or more States, or Parts of States, without the Consent of the Legislatures of the States concerned as well as of the Congress.

The Congress shall have Power to dispose of and make all needful Rules and Regulations respecting the Territory or other Property belonging to the United States; and nothing in this Constitution shall be so construed as to Prejudice any Claims of the United States, or of any particular State.

Section. 4.

The United States shall guarantee to every State in this Union a Republican Form of Government, and shall protect each of them against Invasion; and on Application of the Legislature, or of the Executive (when the Legislature cannot be convened), against domestic Violence.

Article. V.

The Congress, whenever two thirds of both Houses shall deem it necessary, shall propose Amendments to this Constitution, or, on the Application of the Legislatures of two thirds of the several States, shall call a Convention for proposing Amendments, which, in either Case, shall be valid to all Intents and Purposes, as Part of this Constitution, when ratified by the Legislatures of three fourths of the several States, or by Conventions in three fourths thereof, as the one or the other Mode of Ratification may be proposed by the Congress; Provided that no Amendment which may be made prior to the Year One thousand eight hundred and eight shall in any Manner affect the first and fourth Clauses in the Ninth Section of the first Article; and that no State, without its Consent, shall be deprived of its equal Suffrage in the Senate.

Article. VI.

All Debts contracted and Engagements entered into, before the Adoption of this Constitution, shall be as valid against the United States under this Constitution, as under the Confederation.

This Constitution, and the Laws of the United States which shall be made in Pursuance thereof; and all Treaties made, or which shall be made, under the Authority of the United States, shall be the supreme Law of the Land; and the Judges in every State shall be bound thereby, any Thing in the Constitution or Laws of any State to the Contrary notwithstanding.

The Senators and Representatives before mentioned, and the Members of the several State Legislatures, and all executive and judicial Officers, both of the United States and of the several States, shall be bound by Oath or Affirmation, to support this Constitution; but no religious Test shall ever be required as a Qualification to any Office or public Trust under the United States.

Article. VII.

The Ratification of the Conventions of nine States, shall be sufficient for the Establishment of this Constitution between the States so ratifying the Same.

The Word, "the," being interlined between the seventh and eighth Lines of the first Page, the Word "Thirty" being partly written on an Erazure in the fifteenth Line of the first Page, The Words "is tried" being interlined between the thirty second and thirty third Lines of the first Page and the Word "the" being interlined between the forty third and forty fourth Lines of the second Page.

Attest William Jackson Secretary

Done in Convention by the Unanimous Consent of the States present the Seventeenth Day of September in the Year of our Lord one thousand seven hundred and Eighty seven and of the Independence of the United States of America the Twelfth In witness whereof We have hereunto subscribed our Names,

BILL OF RIGHTS

Amendment I

Congress shall make no law respecting an establishment of religion, or prohibiting the free exercise thereof; or abridging the freedom of speech, or of the press; or the right of the people peaceably to assemble, and to petition the Government for a redress of grievances.

Amendment II

A well regulated Militia, being necessary to the security of a free State, the right of the people to keep and bear Arms, shall not be infringed.

Amendment III

No Soldier shall, in time of peace be quartered in any house, without the consent of the Owner, nor in time of war, but in a manner to be prescribed by law.

Amendment IV

The right of the people to be secure in their persons, houses, papers, and effects, against unreasonable searches and seizures, shall not be violated, and no Warrants shall issue, but upon probable cause, supported by Oath or affirmation, and particularly describing the place to be searched, and the persons or things to be seized.

Amendment V

No person shall be held to answer for a capital, or otherwise infamous crime, unless on a presentment or indictment of a Grand Jury, except in cases arising in the land or naval forces, or in the Militia, when in actual service in time of War or public danger; nor shall any person be subject for the same offence to be twice put in jeopardy of life or limb; nor shall be compelled in any criminal case to be a witness against himself, nor be deprived of life, liberty, or property, without due process of law; nor shall private property be taken for public use, without just compensation.

Amendment VI

In all criminal prosecutions, the accused shall enjoy the right to a speedy and public trial, by an impartial jury of the State and district wherein the crime shall have been committed, which district shall have been previously ascertained by law, and to be informed of the nature and cause of the accusation; to be confronted with the witnesses against him; to have compulsory process for obtaining witnesses in his favor, and to have the Assistance of Counsel for his defence.

Amendment VII

In Suits at common law, where the value in controversy shall exceed twenty dollars, the right of trial by jury shall be preserved, and no fact tried by a jury, shall be otherwise re-examined in any Court of the United States, than according to the rules of the common law.

Amendment VIII

Excessive bail shall not be required, nor excessive fines imposed, nor cruel and unusual punishments inflicted.

Amendment IX

The enumeration in the Constitution, of certain rights, shall not be construed to deny or disparage others retained by the people.

Amendment X

The powers not delegated to the United States by the Constitution, nor prohibited by it to the States, are reserved to the States respectively, or to the people.

AMENDMENTS 11-27

Amendment XI

Passed by Congress March 4, 1794. Ratified February 7, 1795.

Note: Article III, section 2, of the Constitution was modified by amendment 11.

The Judicial power of the United States shall not be construed to extend to any suit in law or equity, commenced or prosecuted against one of the United States by Citizens of another State, or by Citizens or Subjects of any Foreign State.

Amendment XII

Passed by Congress December 9, 1803. Ratified June 15, 1804.

Note: A portion of Article II, section 1 of the Constitution was superseded by the 12th amendment.

The Electors shall meet in their respective states and vote by ballot for President and Vice-President, one of whom, at least, shall not be an inhabitant of the same state with themselves; they shall name in their ballots the person voted for as President, and in distinct ballots the person voted for as Vice-President, and they shall make distinct lists of all persons voted for as President, and of all persons voted for as Vice-President, and of the number of votes for each, which lists they shall sign and certify, and transmit sealed to the seat of the government of the United States, directed to the President of the Senate; — the President of the Senate shall, in the presence of the Senate and House of Representatives, open all the certificates and the votes shall then be counted; — The person having the greatest number of votes for President, shall be the President, if such number be a majority of the whole number of Electors appointed; and if no person have such majority, then from the persons having the highest numbers not exceeding three on the list of those voted for as President, the House of Representatives shall choose immediately, by ballot, the President. But in choosing the President, the votes shall be taken by states, the representation from each state having one vote; a quorum for this purpose shall consist of a member or members from two-thirds of the states, and a majority of all the states shall be necessary to a choice. [And if the House of Representatives shall not choose a President whenever the right of choice shall devolve upon them, before the fourth day of March next following, then the Vice-President shall act as President, as in case of the death or other constitutional disability of the President. —]The person having the greatest number of votes as Vice-President, shall be the Vice-President, if such number be a majority of the whole number of Electors appointed, and if no person have a majority, then from the two highest numbers on the list, the Senate shall choose the Vice-President; a quorum for the purpose shall consist of two-thirds of the whole number of Senators, and a majority of the whole number shall be necessary to a choice. But no person constitutionally ineligible to the office of President shall be eligible to that of Vice-President of the United States.

Superseded by section 3 of the 20th amendment.

Amendment XIII

Passed by Congress January 31, 1865. Ratified December 6, 1865.

Note: A portion of Article IV, section 2, of the Constitution was superseded by the 13th amendment.

Section 1.

Neither slavery nor involuntary servitude, except as a punishment for crime whereof the party shall have been duly convicted, shall exist within the United States, or any place subject to their jurisdiction.

Section 2.

Congress shall have power to enforce this article by appropriate legislation.

Amendment XIV

Passed by Congress June 13, 1866. Ratified July 9, 1868.

Note: Article I, section 2, of the Constitution was modified by section 2 of the 14th amendment.

Section 1.

All persons born or naturalized in the United States, and subject to the jurisdiction thereof, are citizens of the United States and of the State wherein they reside. No State shall make or enforce any law which shall abridge the privileges or immunities of citizens of the United States; nor shall any State deprive any person of life, liberty, or property, without due process of law; nor deny to any person within its jurisdiction the equal protection of the laws.

Section 2.

Representatives shall be apportioned among the several States according to their respective numbers, counting the whole number of persons in each State, excluding Indians not taxed. But when the right to vote at any election for the choice of electors for President and Vice-President of the United States, Representatives in Congress, the Executive and Judicial officers of a State, or the members of the Legislature thereof, is denied to any of the male inhabitants of such State, being twenty-one years of age, and citizens of the United States, or in any way abridged, except for participation in rebellion, or other crime, the basis of representation therein shall be reduced in the proportion which the number of such male citizens shall bear to the whole number of male citizens twenty-one years of age in such State.

Section 3.

No person shall be a Senator or Representative in Congress, or elector of President and Vice-President, or hold any office, civil or military, under the United States, or under any State, who, having previously taken an oath, as a member of Congress, or as an officer of the United States, or as a member of any State legislature, or as an executive or judicial officer of any State, to support the Constitution of the United States, shall have engaged in insurrection or rebellion against the same, or given aid or comfort to the enemies thereof. But Congress may by a vote of two-thirds of each House, remove such disability.

Section 4.

The validity of the public debt of the United States, authorized by law, including debts incurred for payment of pensions and bounties for services in suppressing insurrection or rebellion, shall not be questioned. But neither the United States nor any State shall assume or pay any debt or obligation incurred in aid of insurrection or rebellion against the United States, or any claim for the loss or emancipation of any slave; but all such debts, obligations and claims shall be held illegal and void.

Section 5.

The Congress shall have the power to enforce, by appropriate legislation, the provisions of this article.

Changed by section 1 of the 26th amendment.

Amendment XV

Passed by Congress February 26, 1869. Ratified February 3, 1870.

Section 1.

The right of citizens of the United States to vote shall not be denied or abridged by the United States or by any State on account of race, color, or previous condition of servitude—

Section 2.

The Congress shall have the power to enforce this article by appropriate legislation.

Amendment XVI

Passed by Congress July 2, 1909. Ratified February 3, 1913.

Note: Article I, section 9, of the Constitution was modified by amendment 16.

The Congress shall have power to lay and collect taxes on incomes, from whatever source derived, without apportionment among the several States, and without regard to any census or enumeration.

Amendment XVII

Passed by Congress May 13, 1912. Ratified April 8, 1913.

Note: Article I, section 3, of the Constitution was modified by the 17th amendment.

The Senate of the United States shall be composed of two Senators from each State, elected by the people thereof, for six years; and each Senator shall have one vote. The electors in each State shall have the qualifications requisite for electors of the most numerous branch of the State legislatures.

When vacancies happen in the representation of any State in the Senate, the executive authority of such State shall issue writs of election to fill such vacancies: *Provided,* That the legislature of any State may empower the executive thereof to make temporary appointments until the people fill the vacancies by election as the legislature may direct.

This amendment shall not be so construed as to affect the election or term of any Senator chosen before it becomes valid as part of the Constitution.

Amendment XVIII

Passed by Congress December 18, 1917. Ratified January 16, 1919. Repealed by amendment 21.

Section 1.

After one year from the ratification of this article the manufacture, sale, or transportation of intoxicating liquors within, the importation thereof into, or the exportation thereof from the United States and all territory subject to the jurisdiction thereof for beverage purposes is hereby prohibited.

Section 2.

The Congress and the several States shall have concurrent power to enforce this article by appropriate legislation.

Section 3.

This article shall be inoperative unless it shall have been ratified as an amendment to the Constitution by the legislatures of the several States, as provided in the Constitution, within seven years from the date of the submission hereof to the States by the Congress.

Amendment XIX

Passed by Congress June 4, 1919. Ratified August 18, 1920.

The right of citizens of the United States to vote shall not be denied or abridged by the United States or by any State on account of sex.

Congress shall have power to enforce this article by appropriate legislation.

Amendment XX

Passed by Congress March 2, 1932. Ratified January 23, 1933.

Note: Article I, section 4, of the Constitution was modified by section 2 of this amendment. In addition, a portion of the 12th amendment was superseded by section 3.

Section 1.

The terms of the President and the Vice President shall end at noon on the 20th day of January, and the terms of Senators and Representatives at noon on the 3d day of January, of the years in which such terms would have ended if this article had not been ratified; and the terms of their successors shall then begin.

Section 2.

The Congress shall assemble at least once in every year, and such meeting shall begin at noon on the 3d day of January, unless they shall by law appoint a different day.

Section 3.

If, at the time fixed for the beginning of the term of the President, the President elect shall have died, the Vice President elect shall become President. If a President shall not have been chosen before the time fixed for the beginning of his term, or if the President elect shall have failed to qualify, then the Vice President elect shall act as President until a President shall have qualified; and the Congress may by law provide for the case wherein neither a President elect nor a Vice President shall have qualified, declaring who shall then act as President, or the manner in which one who is to act shall be selected, and such person shall act accordingly until a President or Vice President shall have qualified.

Section 4.

The Congress may by law provide for the case of the death of any of the persons from whom the House of Representatives may choose a President whenever the right of choice shall have devolved upon them, and for the case of the death of any of the persons from whom the Senate may choose a Vice President whenever the right of choice shall have devolved upon them.

Section 5.

Sections 1 and 2 shall take effect on the 15th day of October following the ratification of this article.

Section 6.

This article shall be inoperative unless it shall have been ratified as an amendment to the Constitution by the legislatures of three-fourths of the several States within seven years from the date of its submission.

Amendment XXI

Passed by Congress February 20, 1933. Ratified December 5, 1933.

Section 1.

The eighteenth article of amendment to the Constitution of the United States is hereby repealed.

Section 2.

The transportation or importation into any State, Territory, or Possession of the United States for delivery or use therein of intoxicating liquors, in violation of the laws thereof, is hereby prohibited.

Section 3.

This article shall be inoperative unless it shall have been ratified as an amendment to the Constitution by conventions in the several States, as provided in the Constitution, within seven years from the date of the submission hereof to the States by the Congress.

Amendment XXII

Passed by Congress March 21, 1947. Ratified February 27, 1951.

Section 1.

No person shall be elected to the office of the President more than twice, and no person who has held the office of President, or acted as President, for more than two years of a term to which some other person was elected President shall be elected to the office of President more than once. But this Article shall not apply to any person holding the office of President when this Article was proposed by Congress, and shall not prevent any person who may be holding the office of President, or acting as President, during the term within which this Article becomes operative from holding the office of President or acting as President during the remainder of such term.

Section 2.

This article shall be inoperative unless it shall have been ratified as an amendment to the Constitution by the legislatures of three-fourths of the several States within seven years from the date of its submission to the States by the Congress.

Amendment XXIII

Passed by Congress June 16, 1960. Ratified March 29, 1961.

Section 1.

The District constituting the seat of Government of the United States shall appoint in such manner as Congress may direct:

A number of electors of President and Vice President equal to the whole number of Senators and Representatives in Congress to which the District would be entitled if it were a State, but in no event more than the least populous State; they shall be in addition to those appointed by the States, but they shall be considered, for the purposes of the election of President and Vice President, to be electors appointed by a State; and they shall meet in the District and perform such duties as provided by the twelfth article of amendment.

Section 2.

The Congress shall have power to enforce this article by appropriate legislation.

Amendment XXIV

Passed by Congress August 27, 1962. Ratified January 23, 1964.

Section 1.

The right of citizens of the United States to vote in any primary or other election for President or Vice President, for electors for President or Vice President, or for Senator or Representative in Congress, shall not be denied or abridged by the United States or any State by reason of failure to pay poll tax or other tax.

Section 2.

The Congress shall have power to enforce this article by appropriate legislation.

Amendment XXV

Passed by Congress July 6, 1965. Ratified February 10, 1967.

Note: Article II, section 1, of the Constitution was affected by the 25th amendment.

Section 1.

In case of the removal of the President from office or of his death or resignation, the Vice President shall become President.

Section 2.

Whenever there is a vacancy in the office of the Vice President, the President shall nominate a Vice President who shall take office upon confirmation by a majority vote of both Houses of Congress.

Section 3.

Whenever the President transmits to the President pro tempore of the Senate and the Speaker of the House of Representatives his written declaration that he is unable to discharge the powers and duties of his office, and until he transmits to them a written declaration to the contrary, such powers and duties shall be discharged by the Vice President as Acting President.

Section 4.

Whenever the Vice President and a majority of either the principal officers of the executive departments or of such other body as Congress may by law provide, transmit to the President pro tempore of the Senate and the Speaker of the House of Representatives their written declaration that the President is unable to discharge the powers and duties of his office, the Vice President shall immediately assume the powers and duties of the office as Acting President.

Thereafter, when the President transmits to the President pro tempore of the Senate and the Speaker of the House of Representatives his written declaration that no inability exists, he shall resume the powers and duties of his office unless the Vice President and a majority of either the principal officers of the executive department or of such other body as Congress may by law provide, transmit within four days to the President pro tempore of the Senate and the Speaker of the House of Representatives their written declaration that the President is unable to discharge the powers and duties of his office. Thereupon Congress shall decide the issue, assembling within forty-eight hours for that purpose if not in session. If the Congress, within twenty-one days after receipt of the latter written declaration, or, if Congress is not in session, within twenty-one days after Congress is required to assemble, determines by two-thirds vote of both Houses that the President is unable to discharge the powers and duties of his office, the Vice President shall continue to discharge the same as Acting President; otherwise, the President shall resume the powers and duties of his office.

Amendment XXVI

Passed by Congress March 23, 1971. Ratified July 1, 1971.

Note: Amendment 14, section 2, of the Constitution was modified by section 1 of the 26th amendment.

Section 1.

The right of citizens of the United States, who are eighteen years of age or older, to vote shall not be denied or abridged by the United States or by any State on account of age.

Section 2.

The Congress shall have power to enforce this article by appropriate legislation.

Amendment XXVII

Originally proposed Sept. 25, 1789. Ratified May 7, 1992.

No law, varying the compensation for the services of the Senators and Representatives, shall take effect, until an election of representatives shall have intervened.

Source: "The Charters of Freedom." http://www.archives.gov/exhibits/charters/charters.html

Resources

If you want to find out more about Deliberative Methodology and US History, check out the following websites:

DELIBERATIVE METHODOLOGY INFORMATION
International Debate Education Association homepage
http://www.idebate.org

National Forensic League
http://www.nflonline.org/AboutNFL.AboutNFL

U.S. HISTORY
1. In Columbus's Words . . .
Christopher Columbus, Beyond the Textbook
http://www.glencoe.com/sec/socialstudies/btt/columbus

The Columbus Navigation Homepage
http://www.columbusnavigation.com

The Internet Guide to Christopher Columbus
http://www.franciscan-archive.org/columbus

Medieval Sourcebook: Christopher Columbus: Extracts from Journal. http://www.fordham.edu/halsall/source/columbus1.html

2. The Colonies
13 Colonies Webquest
http://www.tesd.k12.pa.us/vfms/shaughnessy/process.htm#links

13 Originals
http://www.timepage.org/spl/13colony.html

Social Studies for Kids: The 13 American Colonies
http://www.socialstudiesforkids.com/articles/ushistory/13colonies2.htm

3. Revolution!
The History Place: Prelude to Revolution
http://www.historyplace.com/unitedstates/revolution/rev-prel.htm

John Bull & Uncle Sam: Four Centuries of British-American Relations
http://www.loc.gov/exhibits/british/brit-2.html

Liberty! The American Revolution
http://www.pbs.org/ktca/liberty

4. Articles of Confederation
Articles of Confederation: America's First Constitution
http://www.constitutionfacts.com/index.cfm?section=articles&page=intro.cfm

U.S. Constitution Online
http://www.usconstitution.net/consttop_arti.html

National Park Service: A Multitude of Amendments
http://www.nps.gov/history/history/online_books/dube/inde3.htm

5. Ratification
Observing Constitution Day
http://www.archives.gov/education/lessons/constitution-day/ratification.html

Ratification of the Constitution
http://teachingamericanhistory.org/ratification

The United States Constitution
http://memory.loc.gov/learn/features/timeline/newnatn/usconst/egerry.html

6. Indian Removal
Digital History: Jacksonian Democracy
http://www.digitalhistory.uh.edu/database/article_display_printable.cfm?HHID=638

Fear is Better than Love: Creek Nation (1832-1837)
http://www.arkansasheritage.com/in_the_classroom/lesson_plans/american_indian/
creek.pdf

Friend of the White Man: Chickasaw Nation (1832-1838)
http://www.arkansasheritage.com/in_the_classroom/lesson_plans/american_indian/
chicksaw.pdf

Our Doom is Sealed: Choctaw Nation (1820-1833) http://www.arkansasheritage.com/
in_the_classroom/lesson_plans/american_indian/choctaw.pdf

The Separatists: The Seminole Nation (1832-1839)
http://www.arkansasheritage.com/in_the_classroom/lesson_plans/american_indian/
seminole.pdf

The Trail of Tears: Cherokee Nation (1836-1839)
http://www.arkansasheritage.com/in_the_classroom/lesson_plans/american_indian/
cherokee_lesson_plan01-10-2003.pdf

7. Slavery

The Debate over Slavery
http://chnm.gmu.edu/exploring/19thcentury/debateoverslavery/assignment.php

Slavery and the Making of America
http://www.pbs.org/wnet/slavery

Slavery in America
http://www.slaveryinamerica.org

Teaching Future Historians
http://dig.lib.niu.edu/teachers/econ1-hammond.html

8. Women and Abolition

Abolitionist Movement
http://www.pinn.net/~sunshine/whm2002/abolitn.html

Abolitionist Movement
http://afgen.com/abmovement.html

Women Abolitionists
http://womenshistory.about.com/od/slaveryto1863/a/abolitionists.htm

9. The Lincoln-Douglas Debates

The Lincoln-Douglas Debates
http://www.mrlincolnandfreedom.org/inside.asp?ID=21&subjectID=2

The Lincoln-Douglas Debates of 1858
http://www.illinoiscivilwar.org/debates.html

The Lincoln-Douglas Debates of 1858
http://www.nps.gov/liho/historyculture/debates.htm

10. Reconstruction

America's Reconstruction: People and Politics After the Civil War
http://www.digitalhistory.uh.edu/reconstruction/index.html

Reconstruction: The Second American Civil War
http://www.pbs.org/wgbh/amex/reconstruction

The Reconstruction Era
http://afroamhistory.about.com/cs/reconstruction/a/reconstruction.htm

11. Immigration

New Americans
http://www.pbs.org/independentlens/newamericans/foreducators_lesson_plan_03.html

The Peopling of America
http://www.ellisisland.org/immexp/wseix_4_3.asp

U.S. Immigration
http://www.fordham.edu/halsall/mod/modsbook28.html

12. Turn of the 20th Century Reform
Progressive Era
http://www.eagleton.rutgers.edu/e-gov/e-politicalarchive-Progressive.htm

The Progressive Movement
http://www.u-s-history.com/pages/h1061.html

Progressive Reform
http://regentsprep.org/Regents/ushisgov/themes/reform/progressive.htm

Progressivism (1900–1920)
http://spider.georgetowncollege.edu/htallant/courses/his225/progmovt.htm

Reforming their World: Women in the Progressive Era
http://www.nwhm.org/ProgressiveEra/statuswomenprogressive.html

13. World War I
American Entry into World War I, 1917
http://www.state.gov/r/pa/ho/time/wwi/82205.htm

First World War.com
http://www.firstworldwar.com

The World War 1 Document Archive
http://wwi.lib.byu.edu/index.php/Main_Page

14. Women's Suffrage
Living the Legacy: The Women's Rights Movement 1848-1998
http://www.legacy98.org/

National Women's History Museum: Suffrage
http://www.nwhm.org/exhibits/toc.html

Not for Ourselves Only
http://www.pbs.org/stantonanthony

15. The New Deal
FDR
http://www.washingtonpost.com/wp-srv/local/longterm/tours/fdr

New Deal Network
http://newdeal.feri.org

President Franklin Delano Roosevelt and the New Deal, 1933-1945
http://memory.loc.gov/learn/features/timeline/depwwii/newdeal/newdeal.html

16. Truman and the Atom Bomb
The Decision to Drop the Atomic Bomb
http://www.trumanlibrary.org/whistlestop/study_collections/bomb/large/index.php

Dropping the Atomic Bomb: Historiography
http://www.anzasa.arts.usyd.edu.au/ahas/bomb_historiography.html

Potsdam and the Final Decision to Use the Bomb
http://www.cfo.doe.gov/me70/manhattan/potsdam_decision.htm

17. Rights Revolution
Center for American Women and Politics
http://www.cawp.rutgers.edu

Overview of Civil Rights Legislation, Supreme Court Cases, and Activities
http://americanhistory.about.com/od/civilrights/a/civilrights1.htm

The Supreme Court
http://www.pbs.org/wnet/supremecourt

18. Vietnam
Vietnam: Introductory Essay
http://future.state.gov/educators/lessons/vietnam/43444.htm

Vietnam Online
http://www.pbs.org/wgbh/amex/vietnam

The War in Vietnam, 1965-1968
http://faculty.smu.edu/dsimon/Change-Viet2.html

19. Rights in Wartime
Civil Liberties after 9/11
http://www.pbs.org/now/politics/timeline.html

Civil Liberties in Wartime
http://www.pbs.org/moyers/journal/07132007/civilliberties.html

Lincoln and Civil Liberties
http://www.historynow.org/12_2008/lp2.html